Dedication

There are so many people that I need to thank and I promise I will get to you in future books. For this book, I'd like to thank my mom and dad. I know it wasn't always easy bringing me up. I didn't always realize it at the time, but you gave-up a lot so I could have an amazing childhood.

Thank you for instilling the belief in me that I can do anything I set my mind to. It was your introduction to finance that got me hooked.

Even as I floundered at times, you were always the rock that I could call upon. With the help of your strength I can use my experiences, and my voice to help others crush debt.

Contents

Introduction

This book is about a portion of my profession that I truly love to teach about, but doesn't get the attention that other areas of financial planning receive. In fact, this is often ignored by a lot of fellow professionals because let's face it, we don't exactly make money in this area.

However, if we get back to the roots of why a lot of financial professionals got involved in the industry initially, it was to help individuals. Not just individuals with a lot of money, but everyone so they can live a better life, and get to the stage where they have money. Money not to just pay their bills, but money in savings for an emergency, money set aside for retirement, and money devoted to vacation and other leisurely pursuits.

The burden that money places on individuals is immense. According to a recent study 35% of all couple said that money was the leading cause of stress in their household. This SunTrust study also showed that strong budgeting and saving strategy was the most appealing money-related quality of a partner. It is safe to say that what we find appealing in a partner certainly changes as we get older.

This stress is the number one reason that partners get divorced. The reasons can range from one person being a saver to another person being a spender. It could be that the spending in the household is causing one person to have to work excessively, causing financial stress. Most the time it is simply debt, as bills become due and creditors start to call, the stress becomes too much for the couple to handle and they go their separate ways.

A personal story for me goes back to college. While I was in college I had to work full-time and still managed a full class load. While my parents were supportive of me and helped immensely, there were times when I had to put large purchases on credit. The story is that of many other people I talk to, things were going to change in the future, I was going to make more money and I would simply pay this off. As time went on the debt started to increase, and while I never skipped a payment it seemed to continue to grow.

I didn't lead a lavish life while I was in college. I didn't even live on campus, I lived in my parent's basement to save on cost and commuted to campus every day. Considering that I was working forty hours a week for a major beverage company, I could cover tuition, books, and several other expenses. I even managed to find time for a girlfriend.

Since my work schedule was built around my school schedule I would normally load up on classes Tuesday and Thursday. While they were a long couple of days it allowed me to keep some sense of normalcy in my life. But when you must work at 5 AM, I never adopted the party lifestyle that others in school had, normally starting Thursday night at the bars. Sure, I had my fun, I may have even overindulged at times, but my experiences were certainly different from others, so my money was not going toward partying and booze.

Still my credit card debt started to increase to a couple of thousands of dollars. Now in hindsight, I know it wasn't a lot but it started to bother me, and I was uneasy in how it was increasing. Through all the struggle I went through I did make it to graduation, it wasn't exactly in four years, but I put in the time and effort and made it successfully in accomplishing a business degree from Western Michigan University.

I figure the struggle, the physical labor, the early mornings, the lack of sleep, and the debt would all disappear once I had that degree in my hand. It was certainly a proud moment for me, I still have the picture where I am being handed my diploma, and that grin on my face would not come off for a solid week.

While I felt like I put in the time and deserved a job with a large company, offering a comfy retirement package, would come my way. Despite my best efforts, it didn't work out as planned. I stayed in the same town for a while trying to find work with almost anyone, I just wanted to prove myself. However, I came face-to-face with trying to find a career in the middle of a recession. No one was going to hire a fresh face who was inexperienced. The pressure took a toll on my mental and physical health, and eventually my relationship.

I made a move West to Seattle where I live today. Even when I got to Seattle it was difficult to find a position. The only companies that would call me were retail organizations or other companies talking about their management trainee positions. The economy had companies skeptical about hiring recent graduates, and in hindsight I can't blame them.

Finally, I got a position managing a go kart facility. While I really enjoyed my job, the patrons, and my coworkers I knew it wasn't a long-term solution. It offered, a decent pay, but there weren't any benefits and it certainly wasn't taking me in the direction I wanted to go.

Considering that my mom worked at a Financial Advisor's office growing-up I was always interested in the stock market and how to make money work for you. I can't tell you how many times I watched the move *Wall Street* and wondered if Gordon Gekko was what people were like on Wall Street . Beyond the entertainment, there is the real aspect of the money helping individuals retire and succeed.

Eventually I connected with an investment firm and I went through their initial training and received my Series 7. That was supposed to be the turning point, I was licensed, I could just see the people banging on my door eager to have me help them, all I would have to do is sit back and count the money. I was snapped back to reality in that I didn't have a base of contacts to begin with and starting from scratch was not going to be easy.

The investment firm I started off with did have a starting salary which helped but it was well below minimum wage when you consider the hours, and eventually I had to switch to another job within the industry to help pay the bills. During this trial, I realized I needed to learn more, I needed to build-up a strong base of contacts, and finally I needed to pay off my debt, because it just kept ballooning as I took on more just to survive.

My next job was with a discount brokerage firm. While before I was concentrating on getting clients this position was trial by fire. I was thrown into the mix placing trades and learning about different products in a short period of time. This was perfect for me professionally as it would make me a much better Wealth Manager. While the money I made was much more than before I still didn't have a lot left over after paying my living expenses. It was at this point that I decided to come open with my friends and family.

By this point I had a good group of friends that I hung out with and since I had the weekends off we would get together on Friday night and have a few drinks before hitting multiple clubs. Once you calculate the drinks, the cover charges, food afterwards, and any cab rides I was probably spending a $100 per night. Some weekend we would go out Friday and Saturday night.

I made the decision to pay off my debt and the first step was telling my friends. This didn't stop us from having a good time or even going out, it just changed how we did it. The amazing thing is once I opened-up, they did too, we were now in this together. Instead of going to a bar first we would head to someone's apartment. It is amazing how a 12 pack of beer can cost the same as a drink or two at a bar. We would go out but only clubs nearby so we didn't have to take a cab, and ones that didn't charge a cover, or where we knew the bouncer. We might still grab a slice of pizza or a hot dog from a food vendor but we would skip going to a restaurant. Those nights soon cost just $20 instead of $100.

Next I needed to bring in more money. While I was fast excelling at my position earning steady pay increases and bonuses, I needed more. Still in my 20's, and not needing a lot of sleep, I took up a position with a catering company. I was introduced to the company by a friend and I loved the concept of either accepting or rejecting job shifts, and I wasn't rejecting any initially. In fact, I was constantly begging them for more shifts because the money was good and I saw my debt going down quickly with the extra payments.

The more I worked with the catering company the more responsibility and pay that I got with them until the point I was bartending, serving, acting as a lead (it is like a manager for an event), and driver for the company vehicle, which usually meant an extra two hours of pay because of travel time. Every minute I could work I would.

At my main job with the brokerage firm I was hourly but quickly learning the ropes and given more responsibility. I was also incredibly eager to earn overtime and worked the extra hours when it was allowed. While it didn't happen overnight it wasn't long before I was putting money away into a savings account. I started putting 15% into my 401(K) with a very generous 50% match from the company. After a good year plus of extra effort my debt was paid off. My credit card debt had reached close to $20,000 at its peak and while that isn't much for some people, for someone making $50,000-$60,000 it was a mountain to climb.

The struggle happened for several reasons. There was certainly a good portion of that debt I could have controlled but I just kept telling myself tomorrow I will start getting it paid off. The time to stop careless spending is today. Some of the debt was used for good purposes such as school, items that student loans didn't cover. Some of it was because of my financial circumstances. Debt will occur to almost everyone at some point in time. Regardless of why the debt happened it can be a stranglehold. For years, it was constantly consuming me, and it took a lot of energy to pay it all off.

The feeling you have when you have reached that milestone is incredible. We live in the land of the free and a place of great abundance and opportunity. We are only truly free when we can be financially free, otherwise we are tied to the demands of the creditors. For many years that is how I lived.

When you break free from those bonds and experience life untethered then you are truly free. I made mistakes when it comes to debt. I wasn't always prepared, but I also didn't know. While I took finance classes, accounting classes, read books, and studied diligently, the classes taught in school aren't personal finance. Unless we are given a good lesson growing-up, and my parents did an exceptional job, mistakes will be made and the school of hard knocks comes into play.

The stress that debt placed on me financially, the strain it put on my relationships, the way it made me freeze for a period in my life is why I am so passionate about it today. I enjoy teaching it to young men and women getting ready to enter the real world. I also enjoy working with adults struggling to better themselves. They want a better future for their children, their spouse, and the causes they care about. They know that proper financial planning can provide all of this and more.

One of the most important things that I've learned in my 57 years is that life is all about choices. On every journey you take, you face choices. At every fork in the road, you make a choice. And it is those decisions that shape our lives-Mike DeWine

I Promise I'll Pay

*I've learned that fear limits you and your vision. It serves
as blinders to what may be just a few steps down the
road for you. The journey is valuable, but believing in
your talents, your abilities, and your self-worth can
empower you to walk down an even brighter path.
Transforming fear into freedom-how great is that?-
Soledad O'Brien*

Debt in its simplest form is something, typically money,
that is owed or due. This simple definition pretty much
sums it up. When you think about it we are surrounded
by debt in all the activities that we do. When you wake-
up in the morning and you are cooled by the air
conditioner or heated by the furnace you surrounded by
debt. You make a promise to the power company that
you will pay them money in exchange for energy.
However, unless you are on a level payment plan, you
have no idea how much you owe them until the bill
comes. That is a form of debt.

As you continue your morning and take a nice warm
shower, that is also debt because you owe for the water
you are using. The use of your fridge, the coffee maker,
and even the electricity to charge your smart phone are
all forms of debt. When you turn on your favorite news
channel in the morning that is debt to the cable or
satellite provider. Finally, as you leave your house in the

morning there is the mortgage owed to the bank and a car payment as you drive away. In these examples, we are provided a product or service that we promise to pay for later.

By its very definition, we are constantly in debt even when we don't have any. But to be fair, not all debt is treated the same, and not all debt is bad. As we go through this book we will look at the different kinds of debt, which ones are bad, which ones you want to avoid at all cost, and finally what order to pay off those debts. The order can have a significant impact on your pocketbook and on your credit score.

Consumer Debt

Consumer debt comes in many forms but that is what we will discuss today. Consumer debt is simply debt that is used to fuel consumption instead of investment. This can come in many forms such as credit card debt, medical debt, student loans, personal loans, cell phones, payday loans, and more. The key point to these loans is that they are unsecured, this means that it is your personal word to pay these off. While you may not be happy that you racked-up the debt there is a moral and ethical obligation to repay the money with interest. There might be times where it simply isn't possible to make payments for a variety of reasons and there are proper ways to handle that, we will cover that later in the book.

Credit Card Debt

The most common type of consumer debt and one that is very easy to abuse is credit card debt. At the end of 2016 the average household, according to nerdwallet.com, had an average of $16,061 in credit card debt. On average the household will pay about $1,292 in interest on that debt. According to creditcards.com the average annual percentage rate was 15.07%.

It would be nice if there was one simple formula to determine if you are getting a good deal on your credit card. Depending on what you are looking to accomplish you will find a lot of different features for credit cards. If you are in a position where you are paying off your balance every month, then you might look for a card that rewards you for things that you want in life. For example, if you enjoy traveling you might get a card that earns you points at your favorite hotel. There are cards that earn you dollars toward your favorite store, airline, cash back, and almost any other reward you could dream about.

If you want to take advantage of credit card perks you still have a to have a good credit score. This will be the primary driver in determining the interest rate that you are charged and the credit limit you are allowed. If you are young unfortunately you may have limited options regardless of how well you manage your finances. This is simply because there isn't a credit history for creditors to judge you. There are however many starter credit cards that will provide you with a card, albeit with a limited spending cap and a higher interest rate. Remember to try to pay it off every month.

The credit score will be a primary driver in the decision that creditors will make on providing you with a credit card. The credit score itself is composed of different factors. It is important to know these factors and use them to your advantage as you make credit decisions. The impact each category has on your credit score varies from high impact meaning that it is very influential, to low impact which has a minimal impact on your score:

- Credit utilization- This is percentage of how much of your revolving debt you are currently using. This can provide the lender with an opportunity to see if you are using your money responsibly. This also give them an indication of how much cushion you have should an emergency come-up. The formula is basic, if you have $30,000 of credit card limits available and you are using $16,000 your credit utilization is 53.3% ($16,000/$30,000). This would be a poor utilization rate and lenders don't like seeing it that high. The ranges they look at include:
  - Excellent is 0%-9%
  - Good is 10%-29%
  - Average is 30%-49%
  - Poor is 50%+

Simply paying a little bit extra off your credit card could boost your credit score by 20 points or more!

- Payment history-This is a huge factor in your credit score and the key here is to simply pay your bills on time. While there is a range, anything less than 96% of your bills being paid on time will result in a poor rating and have a big impact on your credit score. Even when times get tough and you might have to borrow to make a minimum payment make sure to do it. While we hope to avoid that and we'll have steps by the end of this book, please make all your payments

- Derogatory marks (public records)-These are negative marks on your credit report that tend to stay for a long period of time. While you want to avoid these at all cost they can happen. In fact, there are times when it may be healthy for you to go the route to provide yourself a fresh start. However, the impact of derogatory marks can last up to ten years and will require some belt tightening. The most common derogatory remarks include
  - Bankruptcy-This means you have started a proceeding to either reorganize your debt or start a liquidation process to pay your creditors. The most common types of bankruptcy include:
    - Chapter 7-Will eliminate most unsecured debt, any nonexempt property will be sold. Debtors will keep all or most of the property and your house will fall into foreclosure.
    - Chapter 13-You repay your creditors, some in full, some in

part. The repayment plan can last up to five years. You can make-up past house payments and maintain living in your home

- o Foreclosure-This is when you fall behind on mortgage payments and the lender has started legal proceedings. It often takes several months before a lender will start the foreclosure process, they want to work the homeowner to keep them in their home.
- o Collections-These are accounts that have been reported as sent or sold to a third-party collector. In this situation, the original creditors couldn't collect and opted to sell the debt to a third party.
- o Tax liens-These occur when you fail to pay taxes. This can be personal income, property, state, county, or other taxes. While many items fall off a credit report these remain on the report until they are paid off.
- o Civil judgment-This is usually the result of a civil lawsuit where you are required to pay damages and have not done so.
- Average age of accounts-This is a medium impact event on your credit score. This is really where it hurts younger applicants. This is where creditors want to see a history for the accounts that you do have open. In fact, the average range they are looking for includes:

- Excellent is 9+years
- Good is 7-8 years
- Average is 5-6 years
- Poor is less than 5 years
- Total open accounts- This is a low impact event so I wouldn't try to open a bunch of account just to get into the excellent category. Here creditors want to make sure you can manage your finances with multiple accounts. Again, the impact on your credit score is minimal so I don't want any emails about how you filled out 20 loan applications based on this information.
  - Excellent is 21 plus accounts
  - Good is 11-20 accounts
  - Average is 6-10 accounts
  - Poor is 0-5 accounts
- Hard Inquiries- This is another low impact event. These occur when a lender looks at your credit report for a lending decision. This could be for a *mortgage, car loan, credit card, or even getting a cell phone. Since it is a low impact event it will* have minimal impact on your overall score. You may also notice on your credit report soft inquiries. These are done without your permission and can range from employers doing a background check to current lenders making sure you still have solid credit.

It is vitally important to stay on top of your credit report and now there are more ways to do this than ever before. You have the free report that you can get on www.annualcreditreport.com, this was the first big push by the government to make sure that everyone had fair, free, and equal access to their credit report. While this does a good job of showing your credit report, it doesn't provide a credit score. Since annual credit report was made available almost all major banks offer free credit reporting. This includes but certainly not limited to Wells Fargo, Chase, Bank of America, Capital One, and more. In addition, there are online resources that provide you with a free credit score including www.nerdwallet.com, www.wisepiggy.com, www.creditkarma.com, and more.

Like a lot of things in life, even if you have great credit, the more bells and whistles that you want in a credit card the more you are going to pay for it. A credit card that offers rewards such as mileage, a concierge service, and is exclusive can cost a lot. American Express offers the Centurion card to exclusive members who spend $500,000 per year (other reports are $450,000), it has an initiation fee of $5000 and an annual fee of $2500. While this card comes with some great perks and an aura of prestige, it is probably more than what most people need.

More useful would be the Chase Sapphire card with a $95 annual fee but it is consistently ranked as one of the best travel cards. This card happens to have flexible benefits so you aren't tied to one airline or hotel. However, if you fly almost exclusively with one airline or stay at one branded hotel it is usually beneficial to go with that card. These cards also tend to have a higher interest rate to make up for the perks that they are providing for their card holders. If you are paying off your card every month these can be very beneficial. Just make sure the benefit you are receiving is higher than the cost of the card.

If you are looking for a low-cost option you can always check on www.bankrate.com, www.creditcards.com, or several other websites that will provide a comparison for you based on your credit score. There are several cards out there that don't charge an annual fee and can provide a good option. If you are reading this and want to get out of debt, and you are thinking about a balance transfer, than you can search for credit cards with the best balance transfers. I know there are advisors who are rolling their eyes at me for suggesting balance transfers. My thought process is if we can get you into a lower interest rate, save you money, and develop a plan to pay off your debt faster I am all for it.

That little thing about credit scores that we covered. The difference between having an excellent credit score (720+) instead of a poor score (less than 640) can be 10% or more. If you are really struggling with your credit you can get a secure card. With a secure card, you must put down a deposit with the card company, generally equal to the credit limit. You pay the card every month just like a normal credit card, except the credit card company has your money to back the card balance, eliminating the risk. After 6-12 months, the credit card company will revisit your credit and potentially offer an unsecured card.

Just like all the debt that we review you want to use credit cards responsibly. They can be used as a tool to help establish good credit, earn rewards, and come in handy for short-term financial needs.

Since we talked about credit cards and your credit score lets go over some myths:

- o I should close accounts I don't use.
  - ▪ False. We know this for three reasons:
    1. The age of your accounts influences your credit history
    2. This would negatively impact your utilization rate (assuming you have debt)
    3. The total number of open accounts impacts your score
- o Checking my credit score will reduce my score.
  - ▪ False. Looking at your credit score is a soft inquiry, you are entitled to know your score without it impacting you. Hard inquiries will have a negative impact (low impact event).
- o My income affects my credit score.
  - ▪ False. The amount of money you make doesn't have an impact. Your credit score is based on your credit worthiness and your ability to pay your bills on time. The statistics behind it don't care if you make $30,000 or $300,000.

- ○ I don't need a loan so I don't need to worry about my credit.
  - ▪ False. Even if you aren't seeing your doctor you still need to be concerned about your health. Your credit isn't about just today but about your needs tomorrow. If you needed a loan would you be able to get it?
- ○ My score is locked in for 6 months
  - ▪ False. Your score is updated as soon as data is sent into the reporting agency. Your score can change daily, weekly, or monthly.

Ultimately, we want to minimize the amount of debt we have. When we do have to borrow let's make sure it is being done in a manner that is cost effective and makes sense for our personal bottom line.

A word of caution about credit card debt and using it properly. I have a client, we will call him Joe. Joe does well for himself now but his story started like many others. He got his first credit card in college. At the time colleges allowed credit card companies on campus and for a token prize, maybe a nerf basketball, he can't remember why he signed-up for his first credit card.

Initially Joe was diligent about paying it off every month and since it has a low limit of $1,000 it isn't like he could go crazy. This went on for several months until Joe ran into some car trouble, not wanting to beg for money from his parents Joe simply swiped his credit card and paid for the $800 bill that way. Oddly he didn't feel any remorse, any shame, or anything at all, it felt normal to him.

Knowing he was close to his limit Joe called the credit card company to express his concern and to his surprise they raised the limit to $3,000. He had a sense of pride about what had happened, like he deserved this money and was going to spend it. While he still showed restraint he slowly started making bigger purchases. First it was a new laptop, because it was for school, next was a new TV for his dorm room.

Slowly the balance starting to go up but he was diligent about making a payment even if it was just the minimum. Once the balance passed $2,000 he received a letter from his credit card company, because of the responsibility he has shown in making payments they increased his limit to $5,000.

Now it became a card for pizza parties, beer, and entertainment. Joe said he felt good about it, everyone loved being around him. Soon his dorm room was the place to be, with a great stereo, TV's, the latest DVD's, plenty of food. Even his car got some upgrades with a new CD player and loud speakers to match. Being a business major he knew that financing all of this didn't make sense but he figured he would make a lot of money graduating and figure it out.

Soon his card reached its $5,000 limit and needing some new funds Joe applied for a new card to transfer his balance. The new card was eager to assist and transferred all $5,000 at 0% for 12 months with a 3% transfer fee and he still had an additional $1,800 limit he could still use. He was now back in business with $6,800 total credit limit.

This time Joe said he would be responsible and would work hard to pay off the card. Since he was just working a few hours a week and that barely covered his current expenses he needed a way to make more money. He figured he would start his own online company, since so many people were doing that anyway.

Using the available credit limit, Joe created a website. This was going to connect student from his University together so they could buy and sell items. For a nominal cost, someone could post an item for sale and connect with a fellow student. Knowing he had 40,000 students and many of them flush with money he got started.

The website was basic, he got all his business licenses and started marketing. This cost a couple of thousand dollars in flyers, website marketing, and email campaigns. Unfortunately, Joe had his Universities name all over his website and was quickly shut-down for violating licensing agreements.

After a visit to the Dean's office, and a promise to not violate the Universities licensing agreement, he was back at coming-up with ways to make money. He saw an ad in the back of the newspaper about selling t-shirts. He called the company and was informed that if he submitted a design they would print out the t-shirt. The more he ordered the less it cost and the more profit he could make. He used what little remaining credit he had on purchasing t-shirts.

He had connections in fraternities at the University and came-up with some clever designs to sell during Greek week. He ordered around 500 shirts at $5 apiece, he figured he could sell them for $10-$20 and make a nice profit. While sales were robust initially and word spread of the great design, he ran into trouble again. Again, it was for violating licensing rights with the University since he used their logo. He could have also got into trouble for not having a license but the University looked the other way.

The school was now on the verge of kicking him out for multiple violations. Instead they asked for the profits from the shirts and let him finish out his last two years.

Now he had two cards maxed out and applied for a third just to be able to survive. Oh, and the car that he added all those valuable features to eventually died and so he ended up using public transportation his final year. Instead of enjoying his senior year, Joe found himself working multiple jobs just to make the payments on all his debt.

By the time he graduated Joe had $17,000 in credit card debt, and over $30,000 in student loans. This was his wake-up call to the real world. While those years are behind him, he hasn't forgotten the lessons they provided. Joe still uses credit cards today, but he pays them off every month. He also owns a couple of very successful businesses and is a generous donor to his University.

This is an example of misusing balance transfers and misusing credit in a responsible manner. As you go through this book make sure you know yourself, we want to end the cycle of being tethered to the debt chain. If you can't control your spending, look to other methods and we will cover those in future chapters.

Medical Debt

We live in an amazing country where we have access to incredible medical treatments. In fact, some of the wealthiest people from around the world travel to the United States to receive medical treatment. Unfortunately, it seems like one needs to be wealthy to receive treatment in the United States. According to a poll conducted by NPR, The Robert Wood Foundation and Harvard's T.H. Chan School of Public Health nearly 26% of people said that health care expenses caused a serious financial problem.

In fact, medical debt is the number one cause of bankruptcies in the United States. Even as healthcare is being offered to everyone regardless of preexisting conditions, we are still seeing a surge in medical debt. This is for several reasons. One of the main reasons is that companies are being forced to shift more of the health care cost to employees. According to the Kaiser Family Foundation between 2005 to 2015 health insurance premiums for families rose 83%. Between 2006 and 2015 deductibles for individuals increased 255%. This is far higher than wage growth and anytime you have increases this large it is going to hurt the lowest wage earners the hardest.

Why is medical care so expensive in the United States? In an interview with Harvard's David Cutler, an expert economist on health noted several reasons:

1. Administrative cost in the USA accounts for about a quarter of all cost, this is far higher than any other developed country. Our complex system of billing, insurance, and regulations adds to cost
2. Drug costs are higher than in other countries. This is because of everything from the branding of the drug to the lack of leverage used in purchasing the drug.
3. Americans receive more medical care than those in other countries

While not specifically discussed, in other studies it found that Americans tend to receive more medical care partly out of concern of being sued. This means that there will be more MRI's, X-rays, and other medical procedures ordered compared to other countries. The fear of litigation tends to drive a lot of businesses.

We know that medical care is expensive and it probably isn't going to get better. To deter individuals from going to their doctor or other health providers, unless necessary, you are going to see more companies go to a high deductible health care plan. So, what can you do as a consumer to keep your cost down?

o Try to stick with doctors who are in-network- This alone can save you hundreds of dollars.

o Call your insurance provider-Let your insurance provider know what needs to be done, ask how much they cover, and make sure the provider is in-network

o Shop around- Just like hunting for that great deal at Christmas, you can also call around to different hospitals, clinics, and doctors' offices. If you know the procedure that needs to be done they will let you know the price.

o Save money in a Health Savings Account (HSA). These are available for those enrolled in a high-deductible health plan (HDHP). Unlike the Flexible Savings Account (FSA), HDHP's can roll over from year-to-year and can be tax advantageous.

o Stay healthy- This might sound funny but start treating your body like it is the most expensive investment you have, because it is! Exercise a few times a week, eat more salad, and take small steps to a better you.

o Travel- If the expense for a major operation or procedure is too much, look to travel. Sometimes this might mean another country (make sure the hospital has international accreditation) or to another part of the United States. You can often save

70% just by having your procedure done in a smaller city.

If you have gone through all those steps and still find yourself in medical debt there are steps you can take:

- Call the insurance company and make sure the procedures covered. Hopefully you called ahead of time, but if you didn't, an insurance company may still cover the procedure. I have worked with multiple clients whose insurance covered the procedure but the insurance company was billed incorrectly. They simply had to call their doctor's office and have it rebilled. Yes, this is frustrating, and yes it takes a long time but this can save you thousands of dollars.

- Let the hospital know right away that you received the bill and you cannot afford it. Non-profit hospitals are required to offer financial assistance programs. For profit hospitals would still like to see some money rather than none. They will often negotiate a payment program and often reduce the size of the bill. If you have ever seen a bill before it was negotiated by insurance, you know there is a lot of room for negotiating, don't accept the initial amount billed.

- Look at low cost loan options that would pay the bill, and allow you to make payments over a long period of time. This can be a HELOC, personal loan, or other options discussed later.

You want to avoid bankruptcy and use it only as a last resort. Simply ignoring the problem won't make it go away. The best option is to become involved immediately in coming up with a resolution that works with your budget.

"Medical debt is awful, but it could never happen to me." I have heard this from several clients and advise them on the diligence they need to do before any care is provided. Even if you go through all that diligence you might have care that is unexpected and out of necessity you simply go to the nearest facility.

I had a client who did their diligence in that they called their insurer ahead of time about a procedure and they made sure their surgeon was in-network limiting their out-of-pocket expenses. The insurance company assured them the surgeon was in-network. When they received their bills, they found out the anesthesiologist was out-of-network, and they had to pay $16,000 out-of-pocket.

I've also dealt with lower wage earner who got into an accident. While they recovered quickly, their deductible was $10,000. On top of the $10,000 they still had co-pays that needed to be met. The bills continued to pile on. Even though they were both employed, and had insurance through their work, this one accident destroyed years of savings.

If you are presented with any of these situations to someone who is already financially on the edge it is easy to see how medical debt can throw someone into bankruptcy.

Cell Phone Debt

Cell phone debt is becoming more of an issue and carriers are wrapping more into the bills than ever before. This includes the cost of leasing a cell phone, the minutes, data, extras such as voicemail to text and even buying gift cards for others via text. I am sure by the time this is read that phone companies will find more ways to add cost to the bill. As the cell phone has become a much needed and integral part of everyone's life we are seeing more of these bills going to collections.

In fact, cell phone bills are the number two most common items pursued by debt collectors at 37%, medical bills are number one at 59%. So why is it that people don't pay their cell phone? There isn't a clear-cut reason, in fact many people pay their cell phone bill over rent or mortgage because they like to stay connected. The reasons behind not paying can be several. One is a friend, relative, or someone else made unauthorized charges and the owner of the phone doesn't feel like they should pay if the phone company doesn't remove the charges. Sometimes it is simply the cost, the person making the purchase isn't aware of everything they signed-up for and the total cost per month. Other times someone may leave the country and not be aware of roaming charges. Another big one is when someone leaves one phone company for another and simply stops paying on their other phone. Whatever the reason I suspect we will see increased cases of cell phone debt in the future.

The key with cell phones like other debt is to know your limits. There are a lot of plans and a lot of traps out there. Companies like to sell expensive phones attached to their plans saying it will only add $30 per month to your plan over the next two years, or they'll sell you insurance, upgrades, more minutes, more data and almost anything else. In 2015, the average person was paying $110 per month for their cell phone bill, that works out to over $1300 per year and the average amount just continues to go up every single year. Think hard about what is important to you and if you can cut back on some features. If you phone is your entire entertainment package and you are glued to it, that can be a lot to ask. But if you are using it for phone calls and texting only, switch to a plan that would cut your bill in half and put $600 in your pocket.

Utility Bill Debt
Utility bills are the third highest bill sent to debt collectors. This concerns me because there are a lot of resources on a federal, state, and local level to help individuals keep their power on and pay their bills. If you are in danger of having your heat or water turned off and it is a critical situation please check out your states benefits at www.benefits.gov. Call your local provider and explain the situation. Believe me the last thing they want to do is cut off the heat when the temperature is starting to drop.

The federally-funded program that helps low-income households with their energy bills is called LIHEAP (low income home energy assistance program). They can be found by doing a Google search or calling 202-401-9351.

Just looking locally, the city of Seattle has ELIA (Emergency Low Income Assistance), Project Share, HomeWise and more. The worst thing you can do is put yourself in danger and your family in danger by not acting. If you know someone who could use assistance please assist them in taking corrective action immediately.

Many of the collection stories that I have heard about utility bills could have been corrected with some basic actions. Whenever you move make sure you call all your providers and let them know the last day you will be at your current residence. During this time provide them with a forwarding address so they can send you the final bill. This is the number one cause of utility bills going to collections, people simply don't inform their providers of changes. Do this exercise even if your landlord says they will make the call. I have seen multiple cases where the name was never changed and the new resident just racked up cable, heating, water, and garbage bills without ever paying them, because they weren't in their name. While you can plead your case with the utility provider, it is your responsibility to get everything out of your name, the new tenant can worry about it getting it in their name.

Simple steps will save a whole lot of hassle in the future. A half an hour to an hour on the phone sure beats multiple bills going into collections.

Student Loan Debt
Student loan debt is a problem and it continues to grow at an alarming pace. In 2017, the total level of student loan debt stands at $1.41 trillion. This includes 44.2 million Americans with student loan debt. Considering that there are approximately 230 million adults living in the United States, that mean about 20% of the adult population is being dragged down by student loan debt.

I am a big proponent of education and I encourage individuals to expand their horizons. College is an incredible opportunity to expose yourself to individuals, thoughts, and subjects that you would never broach on your own. However, I think too much emphasis has been placed on going to college at any cost.

Before taking on student loan debt it is generally a good idea to do a cost-benefit analysis of what you want to do and the benefit you would receive from it. Right now, the average college student leaves with over $37,000 of debt. Depending on what you want to do that may be more than you want to bite off. What do you have to take into consideration for your analysis:

- Time-College can take 4 years or more, this could be time earning money working, learning a trade, and by going to college you will have to make-up for this later

- Effort- College is what you make of it, with new found freedom you may sleep in without your parents there to wake you up, you can skip classes. There will also be a stretch of classes that may not be pertinent or interesting to you.
- Employment opportunities- Generally a college degree will open-up more opportunities for employment especially for degrees revolving around research. However, many jobs are unfilled such as electricians, plumbers, and welders.
- Earnings- According to a Census Bureau report a college graduate can expect to earn $1.3 million more than a high school graduate. That is a significant amount of money to make.
- Personal development- College just isn't about making more money it is about becoming a better version of yourself.
- Networking- Anytime you can be around other professionals and expand your center of influence it is a positive.

From what I have said it may seem like a no brainer, going to college would be the most sensible solution. There are other factors to consider. Foremost is that not everyone wants to work in an office. Vocational or trade school is a great option for someone who enjoys working with their hands. I know several people who make six figures working as welders, mechanics, plumbers, electricians, and contractors. There will always be a need for someone to fix all our stuff, and why not get paid while you learn the trade.

There are also other people who work in business, as entrepreneurs, and those who are tech savvy who could benefit from real life experience instead of theory in a classroom. If you look at some of the wealthiest people alive, many of them either dropped out or decided to forgo college to pursue their passion.

Also, look at the payout of the profession you are choosing. While I encourage you to follow your passion, just do it is sensible manner. There are several degrees that play an important role in society, but simply don't pay a lot of money. This ranges from social workers, communication majors, psychology (unless doctoral), hospitality and others. It isn't hard to find the mean salary of any profession by doing a simple search online. If you want to pursue a degree in one of those subjects, please do so. But when you are choosing a college find one that is public, low-cost, and can help you find employment. When you start making $40,000 the last thing you need is $200,000 of student loan from a private institution. Ask yourself, would your education at the private college make a big difference in your long-term earnings potential? If it doesn't, than go for a more sensible costing education. Seek out value for your educational dollars.

Think hard about your choices. If you haven't started college yet, and you aren't sure what you want to do, think about going to a community college to complete your prerequisite courses. This can cost a fraction of a Universities cost and when you receive your diploma there isn't an asterisk on the bottom saying you went to a community college, but your wallet can feel the difference.

If you are currently in student loan debt and you are looking for ways to get out, lower, or have part of the loan forgiven there are some choices. One thing to keep in mind with student loans is that regardless of whether you finished your education, whether you found a career in your field, or if you found the education helpful, you are still liable for the debt. Only in extremely rare circumstances is student loan forgiven in bankruptcy. This is part of the reason why so many lenders are willing to take on the risk of student loan debt

Public Service Loan Forgiveness is a program that forgives the remaining balance on your student loans after you have made 120 qualifying monthly payments. With this program, it doesn't matter what your job title is simply that you work for a government organization (federal, state, or local), or for a not-for-profit 501(c)(3). However, if you work for a labor union, partisan political organization, or non-exempt non-profit you are disqualified.

To qualify, your loan must be received under the William D. Ford Federal Direct Loan Program. The big catch is that the payment must be made under the income-driven repayment program (more about this is in a minute). If you aren't sure which student loan you have you can always check your statement or call your provider and they will inform you. You can also consolidate your loan into the program needed to qualify. You must work full-time (30 hours) to qualify. The first of these loans will start being forgiven in October of 2017 since this is a relatively new program for those with loans after October 2007.

Teacher Loan Forgiveness is a program designed to encourage teachers to teach in low-income school districts. There is an annual directory of schools that qualify, this information can be found at www.tcli.edu. To qualify the loan must have originated after October 1st, 1998, the loan can't be in default, and you must work for five consecutive years. Highly qualified teachers, meaning they have a state certification and hold a license in the state they teach, are eligible for up to $5,000 in loan forgiveness. For highly qualified teachers that teach math, science, or special education can receive up $17,500 in student loan forgiveness.

Closed School Discharge is a program that will discharge your federal student loans if the college you are attending closes. This is relevant since ITT and Corinthian just shut their doors leaving thousands of students with unfinished degrees. You must have either been enrolled or withdrew from classes within 120 days of the school closing. Also, if you simply transferred your credits to another school to finish your degree you will no longer be eligible.

Income-based repayment is a program that caps your student loan payments based on your discretionary income. The cap is 10-15% based on when your loan went in effect, those prior to 2009 were capped at 15%, after 2010 is dropped down to 10%. Most federal student loan programs are eligible. After 20-25 years, the remaining balance of your student loan is forgiven. Please keep in mind that currently under federal tax guidelines the amount of the loan that is forgiven is taxable as current income. Depending on the amount of the loan that is forgiven it could result in a large tax bill that year. The process for applying is relatively simple, you must apply online at www.studentloans.gov. This will take you step-by-step to see if you are eligible and let you know what documentation is required.

Many other programs are available to assist individuals with their student loans. Beyond the programs discussed, there are programs to help disabled persons have part or all their student loans discharged. On a state level, there are several programs to assist with students who pursue careers in nursing, medical field, dental, law, and several other areas. The idea behind these is to encourage individuals to work in low-income, underserviced areas that typically wouldn't be a draw to graduates. This can provide an opportunity to reduce your debt and fulfil civic duty.

If you have gone through these programs and don't think you would be eligible, you still have some options. One option is to consolidate your loans with a federal or private lender. When going through this process it can allow you to do a couple of things. One is that it's possible to reduce your interest rate, saving you hundreds or even thousands of dollars. The other option is that it could extend your payments. While this may end up costing you more money in the long-run it could be a smart move. The lowering of payments could free up additional money to pay off higher cost debt. Keep in mind that student loan interest, up to dollar limitations (currently $2,500), is tax deductible lowering your actual interest rate. Once your other debt is paid off, and hopefully you are now making more money, you can concentrate on paying off your student loans early instead of waiting for the length of the loan.

If none of the following situations apply to you and you are in a situation where you can't make a payment, student loan providers will provide you with an option to defer your payment, this is known as deferment. This is simply the process of pausing your current payment until a future date. There are reasons you would be eligible for deferment, they include:

- At least half-time study at a postsecondary school
- Study in graduate fellowship program
- Study in approved rehabilitation training program for the disabled
- Unemployment

- Economic hardship
- Active duty during a war or other military operation/national emergency
- Reserve member of the Coast Guard or other military branches called to active duty while enrolled at least half-time in school. This includes 13 months after returning from active duty, or until the borrower returns to enrolled student status at least on a half-time basis.

If the student loan is subsidized, interest does not accrue during this deferment, however if you have an unsubsidized loan, interest will continue to accrue during the deferment. Deferment is a right of the loan holder, meaning that if you meet eligibility requirements you can defer part of your loan.

Another option is called a forbearance. Forbearance is like deferment in that you delay making payments to your student loan. The main difference here is that the forbearance is not a right of the loan holder. In this circumstance, you must go to your lender and explain why you need forbearance and for what period of time. Many lenders will have eligibility for forbearance listed on their website or provide the reasons if you call them. In all cases of forbearance, the interest that you aren't paying will be added to the principal amount of your loan. While it is nice to not make payments, you are just adding to the total amount owed with each month passing.

There are several nightmare stories that you read about when it comes to student loan debt. I had such as client, we will call her Susan. Susan graduated with a degree in performing arts and is a fine actress. Unfortunately, Susan got her degree at a private college and had over $150,000 in student loan debt when she graduated. Despite being an outstanding actress and talented in many areas, there is a big discrepancy between the money that the Hollywood elite make and those working in your local theatre. Susan would hustle, she was constantly in one or two productions at the same time and picked-up side work when she had an opportunity. Despite her hustle, it was nearly impossible to keep up on her student loans. To make matters worse most loans today are co-signed by the students' parents. She knows that if she defaults it would be up to her parents to cover her payment.

While we worked together on various solutions she knows that for the next twenty years she will have a payment that could buy you a house in several parts of this country. We are working on programs to bring her recurring income through commercials, modeling shoots, voiceovers, web series, original content, and much more. Much of this she must do on the side while preparing for her current roles in local theatre. While we can't change the past, her advice to others would be to keep student loan debt as low and possible, check out more schooling options, and take a good hard look at your income potential when you leave.

I am also working with another couple. We spent time developing a plan for their current situation, their expenses, and what they wanted out of their living years. We developed a comprehensive plan to have them retire in their early 60's, with the option to work part-time if they wanted. Instead, everything changed when their only child defaulted on their student loans.

Since they had co-signed on the loan, the lender came after them for the payments, they didn't have a choice but to make the $850 payment per month. While they are working with their child to get them to pay, they realize because of career and lifestyle choices that isn't going to happen anytime soon. With this new information, we had to redevelop their retirement plan. Now they must cut back on current discretionary spending and work a couple more years to make-up the difference. Student loan debt can affect people beyond just the student.

Personal Loans
Personal loans can often be confused with credit cards but they are different in several different ways. When you use a credit card the payback period is indefinite based on how often you use it and payment you are making. Once you pay down the balance you can use that available credit again to make a purchase. This is known as revolving debt since there isn't a fixed payment, fixed timeline, or initial balance. With credit cards, you generally have a grace period that allows you to make purchases and pay off the balance without

being charged interest. The chief advantage of revolving debt is its flexibility.

Personal loans on the other hand are fixed in their initial amount, fixed in their payment, their interest rate, and their loan period. Once you decide to take on a personal loan you know that it will be paid off in generally three to five years. Personal loans are paid out in one lump sum, the main purpose is to consolidate higher interest rates such as credit cards into a lower interest rates.

This is a great option for someone who has high interest debt, they are in a position of financial stability, and can pay it off in the time listed, or earlier. This is not a good option for someone who would charge their credit card back-up. Now they would be burdened with the debt from their credit card and debt from their personal loan. Since the period for a personal loan is limited, a borrower will have a much higher payment than their credit card. All of this must be taken into consideration when you are trying to figure out the best way to eliminate debt and minimize the amount of interest you are paying.

Payday Loans
If you are currently making payday loans please take a minute to email me at mmeyers@ignitedaboutfinances.com. There are numerous steps you should take before you get into the vicious cycle of payday loans.

For years' payday loans filled a void in the financial landscape. The nicer term for these institutions is "Alternative Financial Services". Individuals would need a temporary infusion of cash to fix a car, pay for a bill, or even to get medication but didn't always have options. Payday loans were designed as a 14 day advance on your next paycheck. When you get paid again you would go in and payoff your debt along with a small fee. The typical payday loan charges around $15 for every $100 borrowed. While this doesn't sound like a large amount it equates to an annual interest rate of 391%. According to the Consumer Financial Protection Bureau (CFPB) an average payday lender pays $458 in fees to borrow $350 over 5 months.

How does that happen? The answer is simple, in the 14-day timeframe when the money was borrowed, most individual's circumstances haven't changed, so they must renew their loan again paying additional fees. This continues until the borrower pays all the money back sometimes months down the road.

Payday lenders also service the 7% of the population that's not associated with traditional banking. This can be for several reasons. One is that there is a skepticism among part of the population about banks and what they would do with their money. There is also a part of the population, based on where they live, that doesn't have ready access to a bank. Finally, there is a small portion of the population who can't open a bank account because of financial abuse in the past. Even looking past the 7% number, there is still 20% of the population that is underbanked. This means that they have a bank account but still prefer to complete transaction through check cashing, payday loans, money transfers, and pawnshops.

When someone who is underbanked gets their paycheck, they go to their check cashing or payday lender who will gladly check the cash for them. With a phone call verifying that the check is good, they will hand you the cash. Unfortunately, they have a fee for this service and it usually starts around 2%. They may even talk the client into loading their money onto a prepaid debit card so they aren't carrying all that cash. The problem is that the card has a fee to be loaded, a fee to be activated, a fee to check the balance, a fee to withdraw money, and a monthly fee. I understand that businesses need to make money however these practices are predatory to those who don't have financial knowledge. Instead of helping the underbanked many use predatory practices to keep individuals in a vicious cycle. This is typically the poorest segment of America's population and because of the practices used, they will remain the poorest.

There isn't a good reason to get a payday loan. Even as states have put hard caps on interest rates it isn't hard to find a lender from almost any state online. As a borrower, you are giving them direct access to your bank account, and allowing for wage garnishment should you default. While 13% of borrowers only take out one or two loans a year, the majority take out multiple loans sometimes from several institutions, creating an endless cycle that is extremely difficult to escape.

For happiness one needs security, but joy can spring like a flower even from the cliffs of despair- Anne Morrow Lindbergh

I'll Back Up My Promise

Some debts are fun when you are acquiring them, but none are fun when you set about retiring them-Ogden Nash

The debts that we have covered so far has been unsecured debt. This is the riskiest debt taken on by a lender and the most scrutinized on credit reports. When you are dealing with unsecured debt you are relying on the faith of the borrower to pay that money back. The next couple of debts we will discuss are considered secure debt. Secure debt simply means that the loan is backed by something, this can be something physical like a house or car, or something intangible such as a patent or trademark.

Auto Loans
The love affair with the automobile is alive and well today. There is nothing quite like the image of a sports car all shined up with the sun out just hugging the road as it goes around a curve. Better yet, keep that image, have the ocean in the background and a big smile on the owner's face. This illusion of a carefree lifestyle helps to sell cars, car companies want to make us believe that we are an extension of what we drive.

Unfortunately for many people they have extended themselves trying to fulfill that illusion by buying vehicles well beyond what they can afford. So many financial articles focus on the small items, such as a cup of coffee, that add to our daily expenses. I am all about taking small steps to save money, and yes in theory it works, but if that cup of coffee is your break for the day, your little escape I am all for it. I think the first-place people need to look is in their driveway.

In 2014, the median household income was $53,719, this means that half of Americans make more and half of Americans make less. The average price for a new car is $33,560, that means if someone makes the median income they are spending over 62% of their gross income on that purchase. If they pay 20% in taxes that means 78% of their annual income was spent on a car. This is the real reason people are broke, it isn't their latte, it is their vehicle. While I know, everyone needs a safe vehicle to drive, they need to do so without breaking the bank.

How is that someone can afford such a vehicle? When car loans first came out most of them were for three years and 20% down was required. If you could get the vehicle to last 10 years it was a pretty good investment and served its purpose. Car dealers are smart and realized that people buy based on payment, not on price tag. They started to offer 5, 6, 7 and even 9-year auto loans. Are you kidding me?! To compete banks and other financial institutions started to match their time frame. Most banks have capped their term to 6 years, while you can get longer at the dealership.

This is encouraging people to buy cars that would normally be out of their budget by focusing on the payment. With rare exception, the car is a depreciable asset, so it goes down in value, often faster than your car loan. This can be problematic especially if you get in an accident and owe more on the car than what it is worth. Even if you don't have the vehicle, you still must pay off the remaining balance to your lender. Exactly how fast do cars depreciate? They depreciate fast, simply driving a car off the lot brand new will depreciate its value by 11%, after one year it is 20%, three years 46%, and after five years on average your car will have depreciated 65%. That vehicle that you bought for $33,560 is now worth $11,746. This is on average; some vehicles depreciate faster than others.

Now you have been spending money on an item worth far less than what you initially paid While the average age of a modern vehicle is 11.4 years, the average length of time an owner keeps their vehicle is just shy of 6 years. What happens is that we have people now trading in their car for a new one but they still owe money on their old one. Not a problem says the dealership, we will give a trade-in credit and just rollover any remaining debt into the new car payment, keeping the cycle going. You are now upside down on your new vehicle before you even leave the lot, and it is about to depreciate 11% as soon as you take it home.

This cycle of car payments is the real reason you are broke. If you finance a $33,000 car over six years, and you have excellent credit rating, and pay just 2.49% you are looking at monthly payments of $479. If you have two or three cars in your family it is easy to pay over $1000 a month for the shiny vehicles in your driveway.

On top of that someone who buys a new car instead of used ends up paying about $775 more in cost per year. This cost includes higher insurance premiums, registration renewals, and maintenance. These are dollars leaving your wallet that you don't think about. Only when you don't have those extra expenses can you realize the difference.

As a rule of thumb, you will want to spend around 10% of your gross income on your vehicle. Looking at the median income, that would be $5,371, six times less the average new car. In rare cases I allow my clients to increase that amount if they are in debt. Let's face it, we all need a safe vehicle to ride and I don't want you to jeopardize your family's safety. But used vehicles have lost their stigma, and can be reliable lasting for several years. The cost savings can directly help you to lower or eliminate other debts, you can increase your savings, and even provide for more discretionary spending. A $5,000 car financed over three years will only cost you $145 with excellent credit, a much better use of your money.

I understand that this is a touchy topic with several people. If you don't have any debt and you saved up for that one vehicle you have always wanted. The one that cost $60,000 or $100,000, I understand that. There is an emotional attachment to vehicles. In these situations, if an emergency fund is in place and retirement goals are being met I am all for it. Because it was planned and prepared for, and more importantly it was paid for in cash. My goal is to have you crush debt not continue the cycle. If I can save you a $5,000 a year or more by buying a used vehicle that is actual money in your pocket that can get you on the right track to financial success.

Final note on car loans is that these are secured loans. What that means is that your car is collateral against the loan. If you fail to make timely payments the bank can repossess your car. Once a car is repossessed it is sold at auction to help cover their expenses. When a car is sold at auction it is generally well below the resale value. Remember the bank is not in the business of selling cars and it doesn't want to be. After the car is sold, if there is still a difference between the value received and the loan balance, the bank can go after you for the deficiency balance. If you owed $4,000 and they received $750 for the vehicle less a $150 auction fee, the bank can go after you for the $3,400 still owed. At that point in time you can work out a payment arrangement with the bank, pay off the balance, or negotiate a settlement. Each state has their own rules so please reviews your states laws if your car becomes repossessed. In certain situations, depending on the remaining balance, your bank may forgive that balance.

Vehicles represent freedom for a lot of people and with this freedom comes responsibility so make sure you can manage your debt load and pay creditors off in a timely manner.

Mortgage Debt
People will often speak of good debt and bad debt. I agree with this line of thinking. If you can use debt as a means of building wealth than that is using leverage in a positive manner. The same line of thinking that goes along with student loans, if you strategically using it to gain an advantage in your employment and income, that is smart. Burdening yourself with debt that won't produce a net positive for you, the consumer, is bad debt. The same goes with your house.

You can view homebuying in a few different ways. One is that you can try to flip a home like they do on the TV shows. If you watch these shows, the professionals will often have a hard time making a profit, at times they will even lose some money. There are those flips where they make a huge amount of money, those always seem to stick in our mind. If you have never flipped a home before you can always hire a general contractor, they will have the connections to bring all the subcontractors together to complete your work. However, this will add to the cost, most of the flips you see on TV they act as their own general contractor. These individuals have done enough work that they know multiple individuals who do plumbing, electrical, foundation, landscape, and painting to get the work done in a timely manner and with a reasonable cost. If you are paying retail for these services, you can expect to pay more than they do on TV.

You will also notice that many of these individuals have an eye for interior design. This will allow them to envision the finished result with an idea about finishing's, paint color, and trim work. They will know what items add value to the house and what items take away from your bottom line. They also happen to know who has the best value in town for the finishings they want. This includes appliances and other high cost items.

If you are determined to cross this line and flip a house make sure you go in with a good game plan and a lot of cash. Most of the homes are bought at auction without an inspection. You can look at the exterior but after purchasing one you might walk into a house with all the piping ripped out, an uneven foundation, and an electrical system not up to code. You might even discover that the great add-on that makes the house unique from the neighborhood was not permitted. This could cause you to rip the entire section down if an inspector or city refuses to permit it.

While there is risk with flipping a house, there is also the potential for a great reward. There are people who try to do most of the work themselves, they may even live in the house during this process. To them it is a longer flip and a work of love. However, the process can be all encompassing and you must be willing to spend all your free time working on the house.

To those who want to be hands off and just take in the money, let's do the math. First, it is very important to know your local market. That is why many real estate flipper's also work in that local market as a realtor. You will want to find a house that is selling for 20-30% below the retail market. This will provide you with a margin of error for repairs, carrying cost, property taxes, utilities and other unexpected bills.

You have done your homework and found a great property for $150,000 in a market where the homes sell for $200,000 and you decide to make your move. Since this is a flip and you need financing it will likely cost between 10-14%, this isn't likely a conventional mortgage where you are paying 3-4%. Depending on the state of the property you might have to look at commercial loan arrangements, and expect to put a minimum of 20-30% down.

Let's look at potential numbers for this flip. We must pay the carrying cost, the cost of financing the house and using the utilities during the flip. We also must pay closing cost on the purchase and sale. In addition, we still need to fix it.

$	(150,000.00)	Home purchase
$	(4,500.00)	Closing cost (purchase)
$	(4,936.00)	Carrying cost ($120,000 @ 12% over 4 months
$	(1,000.00)	Utility bills
$	(20,000.00)	Repairs
$	(2,000.00)	General contractor
$	(6,000.00)	Closing cost (selling)
$	(188,436.00)	Total cost
$	200,000.00	Selling Price
$	**11,564.00**	Gross Profit
$	(2,312.80)	Taxes (assuming 20%)
$	**9,251.20**	Net Profit

In this example you made money, great job! However, this flip was a relatively short-term flip in that it took 4 months. It isn't unusual for deals to fall through and you must restart the selling process. This project also went smoothly, but if there were some unexpected delays with a contractor or a bigger problem was discovered, you are looking at additional cost. Finally, you could save money by being your own general contractor. You could also act as your own real estate agent where you would save on buying and selling costs. Both options will personally cost you additional time. This is where you put a value to your time and what you are worth.

Looking at your profit in this case it is $9,251 which isn't bad for four months' worth of work. However, if you work in sales or another position where you can work additional hours you must figure how much you make per hour and whether this is worth the risk. If you make

$75/hour when you are selling and you are certain of your ability, you could work an additional 8 hours per week for that same 16-week period to make that money without risking your own capital. However, if you have a 40 hour a week job that doesn't offer the potential to make additional money through overtime or bonus, is this a risk you can afford to take? If you make money flipping the house than you added to your net worth and improved your family's situation. However, if you lost $10,000, is this is a financial blow that you can afford to make? How far back would it set your family's finances?

The reality of flipping isn't like the TV shows. There are professional companies that flip multiple houses a month and they admit that they expect to lose money on a couple, make a little money on a couple, and hit a home run with one or two. If professionals play these odds then it is like rolling the dice as an individual trying to make money this way. Just like anything else, be prepared going into your flip, do your homework ahead of time, try to make projections, and be as strategic as possible.

Another potential way to make money through real estate is by renting out your property. I have spoken with several people who started off flipping a property but because of the economy, the real estate market, or other reasons, they ended up becoming landlords. Renting out your property can become profitable but it is usually a matter of being patient.

Interest rates for financing an investment property will be a couple of percent higher than a traditional mortgage. In addition, you will have to put a minimum of 20% down, if you can put down 25% you may qualify for additional reductions. If you are looking to use the income from the investment property to help you qualify this better not be your first investment property. Most lending institutions will want to see at least two years of property management experience to have that income qualify.

You can make money as a landlord, but a lot of it will depend on your local market, your renters, and unexpected cost. Most homes can be rented out for between .08% and 1.1% of their value. The difference between the two can mean the difference between making a profit and losing money every month. In terms of landlords they will say the property is either cash flow positive or cash flow negative. If a property is cash flow negative then you are paying money out of your pocket every month to cover cost. Conversely a property that is cash flow positive will put money in your pocket every month. Below is an example of a house purchased for $150,000, financing $120,000 at 5.5%. Insurance is the national average, typically there is a 25% premium for investment properties. The property taxes are 1%, which is the national average, maintenance costs are 2%, capital expenditure are 3% which are together under repairs, and property management cost are 10% of the rental income. In this example, the house rents for .08% of its current value.

Income	Mortgage	Insurance	Taxes	Repairs	Management	Profit/Loss
$ 14,400.00	$ (8,176.20)	$ (1,190.00)	$ (1,500.00)	$ (7,500.00)	$ (1,440.00)	$ (5,406.20)
$ 14,904.00	$ (8,176.20)	$ (1,225.70)	$ (1,552.50)	$ (7,762.50)	$ (1,490.40)	$ (5,303.30)
$ 15,425.64	$ (8,176.20)	$ (1,262.47)	$ (1,606.84)	$ (8,034.19)	$ (1,542.56)	$ (5,196.62)
$ 15,965.54	$ (8,176.20)	$ (1,300.35)	$ (1,663.08)	$ (8,315.38)	$ (1,596.55)	$ (5,086.02)
$ 16,524.33	$ (8,176.20)	$ (1,339.36)	$ (1,721.28)	$ (8,606.42)	$ (1,652.43)	$ (4,971.36)
$ 17,102.68	$ (8,176.20)	$ (1,379.54)	$ (1,781.53)	$ (8,907.65)	$ (1,710.27)	$ (4,852.50)
$ 17,701.28	$ (8,176.20)	$ (1,420.92)	$ (1,843.88)	$ (9,219.41)	$ (1,770.13)	$ (4,729.27)
$ 18,320.82	$ (8,176.20)	$ (1,463.55)	$ (1,908.42)	$ (9,542.09)	$ (1,832.08)	$ (4,601.52)
$ 18,962.05	$ (8,176.20)	$ (1,507.46)	$ (1,975.21)	$ (9,876.07)	$ (1,896.21)	$ (4,469.09)
$ 19,625.72	$ (8,176.20)	$ (1,552.68)	$ (2,044.35)	$ (10,221.73)	$ (1,962.57)	$ (4,331.81)

In the above example the house never has a positive return on its investment. We are assuming that housing prices are inflating at 3.5% per year. However, we don't have to look too far back to realize housing prices don't always go up. Depending on the area of the country you are in, you may not be able to increase the rent every year.

Below is the same example with the homeowner able to charge 1.1% of its current value.

Income	Mortgage	Insurance	Taxes	Repairs	Management	Profit/Loss
$ 19,800.00	$ (8,176.20)	$ (1,190.00)	$ (1,500.00)	$ (7,500.00)	$ (1,980.00)	$ (546.20)
$ 20,493.00	$ (8,176.20)	$ (1,225.70)	$ (1,552.50)	$ (7,762.50)	$ (2,049.30)	$ (273.20)
$ 21,210.26	$ (8,176.20)	$ (1,262.47)	$ (1,606.84)	$ (8,034.19)	$ (2,121.03)	$ 9.53
$ 21,952.61	$ (8,176.20)	$ (1,300.35)	$ (1,663.08)	$ (8,315.38)	$ (2,195.26)	$ 302.35
$ 22,720.96	$ (8,176.20)	$ (1,339.36)	$ (1,721.28)	$ (8,606.42)	$ (2,272.10)	$ 605.60
$ 23,516.19	$ (8,176.20)	$ (1,379.54)	$ (1,781.53)	$ (8,907.65)	$ (2,351.62)	$ 919.66
$ 24,339.26	$ (8,176.20)	$ (1,420.92)	$ (1,843.88)	$ (9,219.41)	$ (2,433.93)	$ 1,244.91
$ 25,191.13	$ (8,176.20)	$ (1,463.55)	$ (1,908.42)	$ (9,542.09)	$ (2,519.11)	$ 1,581.75
$ 26,072.82	$ (8,176.20)	$ (1,507.46)	$ (1,975.21)	$ (9,876.07)	$ (2,607.28)	$ 1,930.60
$ 26,985.37	$ (8,176.20)	$ (1,552.68)	$ (2,044.35)	$ (10,221.73)	$ (2,698.54)	$ 2,291.87

What a difference .03% can make in the outcome of a successful transaction. But it is vitally important to know your market and how much you can charge. Some parts of the country you can only charge .05%, which could really change your calculations. These charts also assume that you are renting out your property 100% of the time. We know that isn't realistic. While you might strike the jackpot with renters who stay for years, realistically you will have to find new renters for a single-family home every three years. If you are renting out an apartment it is every year. Finding a good tenant can take a month or longer, while you want to rent it out quickly, you don't want to rent it to the wrong person. You will have a couple of months of no rent, in addition you will have to spend $1,000 or more painting and cleaning the property for the next tenant. This can deduct $5,000 or more during years when you transition to a new tenant. This also needs be taken into consideration,

Another note on rental properties, I see people who fail to put 5% of the rental income away for maintenance and capital expenditures. Maintenance will be the routine actions you need to take to keep your home in its current condition. This will include furnace check-ups, basic repairs, pressure washing, and other routine work. However, capital expenditures will be big projects, this includes a new roof, hot water heater, washer/dryer, furnace, deck, driveway, or a myriad of other home projects. Do yourself a favor and put that money away in a savings account because eventually it will be needed. More landlords must declare bankruptcy or fail to ever make a profit for not considering their capital expenditures. Also, keep in mind, many people will calculate a much higher rate for their capital expenditures, you must be aware of the property, the useful life for many of the high-ticket items and realistically when they will need to be replaced.

As you are looking through the expenses you may decide to save the 10% cost and manage the property yourself. Unless you are in the business of being a property manager, it is usually wise to outsource this task. Usually, after the first or second call at 3:00 in the morning, you will decide that this isn't for you. Most landlords have other professions they excel at and that is where they want to keep their focus. Besides do you want to go on vacation and try to coordinate a major repair while on a beach in Mexico? Leave the management of the property to a trust company.

Renting out real estate can be a rewarding experience, but it is usually served best for those with patience. When you have paid off the property, or owned it for a long-time, you really start to reap the rewards of cash flow positive rental income. The first few years can be challenging as income and expenses remain relatively close. While it's possible to use leverage (debt) to create positive income, make sure you do research on the area to make sure the rent you want to charge is supported so you can make a positive return.

Finally, there is the trusted and true method of buying a home and living in it. While certainly not glamorous, owning a home is an important wealth building step for many people. The process of buying a home is relatively easy, but a major milestone. Getting into a house can require as little as 3.5% down through an FHA qualified loan. Others will require 5% for a conforming loan or a more traditional 20% down.

While I am a proponent for home ownership it certainly isn't for everyone. We are seeing a generation of millennials that are currently shying away from home ownership. They are looking for the flexibility that comes with renting. We are in a fluid society where people will often leave their state or even their country to pursue their careers. When you rent, this provides you with a temporary housing solution so you have flexibility in other areas of your life. There are also others who don't want the maintenance, or financial responsibility associated with a house. There isn't anything wrong with that, just understand your personality and your needs when you consider housing options.

Once you are settled in where you want to live, and believe you will have some permanence, a house is a great wealth building tool. There are several reasons for this. The first is that a house is a forced savings account. Every single month a portion of your payment will go to paying down your principal. As you continue to pay every month, more of the house is officially yours. With additional principal payments, the house will quickly yours. Also, once you lock in your mortgage payment that is it for the life of the loan. The insurance, property taxes, and other costs will continue to rise but your mortgage payment will remain the same. Assuming a regular cost of living increase the cost of living in your house becomes a much smaller percentage of your income as the years proceed. Compare this to renting where you don't have any equity in your residence, and the costs continues to increase every year.

In addition, as the amount of money you owe on your house goes down, the value of your house, under normal conditions, continues to rise. This will increase the amount of wealth you generate.

The temptation with the equity in your home is to use it as a piggy bank. This doesn't encourage careful spending, in fact it encourages you to live well beyond your means. The average household will refinance their house every five years.

There are good reasons to refinance your house. One reason is to lower the interest rate. The important factor here is to look at your long-term cost. Many people will look at their monthly payment drop but not realize they are still paying more over the long-term than if they stuck with their original payment. A better option would to move to a 15-year fixed, get a lower interest rate, a shorter time, and significantly less interest expense. Let's look at our example of the $150,000 house. We will assume 5% was put down on the house and the original mortgage was a conventional 30 year with a 4% fixed rate.

House value	Loan Amount	Interest	Mortgage	30 yr Interest	Difference
$ 150,000.00	$ 142,500.00	4.00%	$ 680.32	$ 102,414.05	
$ 178,152.95	$ 130,176.59	3.50%	$ 584.55	$ 80,261.79	$ 5,054.45
$ 178,152.95	$ 130,176.59	3.00%	$ 548.83	$ 67,402.12	$ (7,805.22)
				15 yr Interest	
$ 178,152.95	$ 130,176.59	4.00%	$ 962.90	$ 43,145.50	$ (32,061.84)
$ 178,152.95	$ 130,176.59	3.50%	$ 930.61	$ 37,333.16	$ (37,874.18)
$ 178,152.95	$ 130,176.59	3.00%	$ 898.98	$ 31,639.02	$ (43,568.32)
Refinancing				30 yr Interest	
$ 178,152.95	$ 142,522.36	4.00%	$ 680.42	$ 102,430.12	$ 27,222.78
$ 178,152.95	$ 142,522.36	3.00%	$ 600.88	$ 73,794.45	$ (1,412.89)
				15 yr Interest	
$ 178,152.95	$ 142,522.36	4.00%	$ 1,054.22	$ 47,237.36	$ (27,969.98)
$ 178,152.95	$ 142,522.36	3.00%	$ 984.23	$ 34,639.63	$ (40,567.71)

- 1% was added to refinance for closing cost
- $27,206.71 was paid in interest the first 5 years before refinancing

As you can see from the chart there are times to refinance, and times to just weigh your options. In the first box, you can see the only reason to refinance would be if mortgage rates dropped an entire percent. In this case, you would save $7805.22 going back into a 30-year mortgage. This would also free up $131.49 per month that you could use to eliminate more costly debt.

Once you start to eliminate the amount of time you have on your loan by switching to a 15-year mortgage, the amount of interest you pay goes down dramatically. The interest rates in this illustration were the same as the 30-year mortgage. You will typically save almost a percent or more by switching to a 15-year mortgage with all things being equal. But just maintaining a 4% mortgage you will save over $32,000 in interest by switching to a 15-year mortgage, assuming you can afford the extra $282.58 per month you will be in a great position financially.

The other chart shows something we are trying to avoid and that is using our house as a piggy bank. I have counseled countless people who think they are doing the right things. They are saving in their 401(K), they bought a house, they have a savings account but they never seem to make progress. Only when you start pulling back the curtains do you see that they habitually take loans on their 401(K), they are constantly refinancing their house to afford their cars and pay off credit card debt. They are caught in a cycle where on the outside things look good, but they are sabotaging their own financial future. How would you feel if you made payments on your house for 15 years only to realize that you don't have any equity? This happens all too often.

In the illustration, we show a second group, and this is for cash-out refinancing. Most people would opt for the 30-year mortgage again since it offers low payments, almost identical to what they had before. Cashing out their house they pay-off debt, and now they feel good about their situation, however in the long-run this will cost them over $27,000 in additional interest. This assumes they hold their new mortgage the whole 30 years, not a likely scenario.

I understand that things do happen and maybe you are trying to consolidate some medical debt, credit card, or you had a string of months where you were unemployed. This could really help to manage your payments and put you on a better path. If this is the case then refinance but just do it one time and ideally into a shorter-term loan so you save on interest. However, if you find yourself habitually refinancing, then it is time to seek help with someone who can help you manage a budget.

A key point to remember, if you are refinancing to consolidate debt, is that the mortgage is a secured loan. If you saw a huge increase in the value of your home, and the refinancing increases your mortgage payment, make sure you can comfortably handle the payment. It is one thing to only make the minimum payment on your credit card for one month and it is something else to miss your mortgage payment. If this happens multiple times you could be in danger of losing your home.

If mortgage rates have risen since you originally purchased or last refinanced your house, but you want to save on interest expenses, you have some choices. One option is to check out a 15-year rate, it still might be low enough that it would save you money. Make sure the rate is ½% lower than your current rate, ideally at least 1% for it to make sense. If those options aren't available for you simply call up your lender and let them know you would like to make an additional principal payment every single month. I don't know of a single lender that doesn't allow this. In this case, you want to pay an extra $282.58, this keeps the interest rate at 4% but will save you over $32,000 in interest expense. This saves you on closing cost from refinancing and helps you to build wealth faster.

One option that I hear touted is to make half of your mortgage payment every two weeks and that will save a few years off your mortgage. While that is true, I am not a big fan of this for several reasons. The first is if you set this up through a bank and you may make a payment every two weeks, but the bank will hold your funds and apply them once a month like you are making a regular monthly payment. The extra payment will only happen at the end of the year after the other 12 payments have been met. Some banks will divide your 12 payments into 26 so you aren't making any real progress toward paying down your house and eliminating that costly interest.

The second reason I am not a fan of the bi-weekly mortgage payment is because many companies will work with a vendor who charges a fee. Now with these programs the payment does get applied every two weeks and it will eliminate the time you pay on your house. However, the bank generally applies your normal principal and interest payments until all 12 are met. Only then will the bank apply the "extra" money toward principal at the end of the year. There is a better option. If you simply call up your lending institution and tell them you want to make an extra principal payment each month of X amount of dollars they will gladly do that.

This will go directly toward your principal each month, save you on fees, save you on interest and typically save you a month or more on house payments over the bi-weekly mortgage plan.

One final thought on mortgage debt is that it isn't always feasible for someone to pay their house off in 15 years. With the current low interest rates, it should be a last priority. There are times when I advise people to go from a 15-year to a 30-year mortgage because it frees up their cash flow. When they have additional money than they can pay down the mortgage. If your money can work harder for you elsewhere, then take advantage of that opportunity.

Having mortgage debt is a reality for many people. If you must have debt at least you get a deduction with your mortgage interest. But please don't use that as an excuse to have a mortgage. If you paid me a $1 in interest and I gave you $.20 paid at the end of the year would you like it? That is what it is like with mortgage interest, it isn't a tax credit, it is a deduction. While nice, I would rather have that entire $1 in my pocket. Just like everything we are trying to do, we want to use debt in a smart manner. We want to make sure that ultimately it is working for us and not against us. We don't like to pay interest, by taking small steps we can minimize the amount of interest we pay and continue to crush debt!

A journey of a thousand miles begins with a single step-Confucius

The race to get out of debt

The discipline you learn and character you build from setting and achieving a goal can be more valuable than the achievement of the goal itself-Bo Bennett

Money, while an inanimate object, can sway emotions greatly. Money can tear apart relationships and cause anxiety. It can allow for a feeling of hope and freedom, or dread and despair. For centuries men have clamored for it, killed for it, and even prayed for it. Little has had such staying power as the lust for money over the centuries. While the form of money has changed over time the results have been the same. We have seen countless monarchs fall because of financial difficulties or financial excess. Even in recent history we have seen countries such as Greece on the verge of collapse because of mismanagement of money. Even in the United States, one of the largest cities, Detroit, had to declare bankruptcy because of a shrinking tax base, reckless spending, corruption, and poor management.

All of this has a real impact on the lives of those living in these areas. When an area is inundated with debt, generally, they will have to raise taxes, implement austerity measures, while simultaneously attempt to promote pro-growth. All of this has an impact on businesses, individuals, and families. The impact is especially felt by those who work for the government. Talk about tough, imagine working for a government that must cut services, increase taxes all the while trying to maintain accountability to its constituents.

Now imagine, or maybe you've experienced it, working for a government at that time. The morale must be low as you go out and try to best represent your city. But as Mr. and Mrs. Taxpayer are paying more for less you are eyed as an expense, a reason that they don't have as much disposable income. While this is happening, you find out that the city has started the process of laying off workers. Friends and colleagues that you have known for years are starting to disappear. Wages have been frozen and in many cases negotiations have started to reduce wages to keep more people employed. As the process speeds up everything you felt secure about is starting to fade away. You soon realize the pension that you thought was secure is only as good as the institution funding it. In fact, because of underfunding and the threat of bankruptcy you may not receive your full pension. Money management affects everyone.

Whether it is governments, corporations, or non-profits they all need discipline and a plan to succeed. Part of the process is being held accountable for their roles and executing. If you have ever looked at an organizational chart you will find this is put into place so there is accountability. The accountability goes all the way up to the CEO or President. The chart is put into place so the company knows who to look for regarding direction and vision. Furthermore, there will be divisional vice-presidents or managers to help make sure each division is run efficiently and with proper guidance. Imagine trying to run a company with 5000 employees and everyone reported to just the CEO or President. They would be overwhelmed by trying to manage so many individuals. Instead processes and people are put into place so big ideas can be generated and the fine details can be worked out by those closest to the client.

In conjunction with the organization chart there will be a "key roles & responsibilities chart". This will produce finer detail of what is expected individually and how they support the organization overall. After all it is difficult to hold someone accountable if you don't know what they are accountable for. This provides a basic over view of how a business is set-up initially. Now just because the company has a great organizational chart, and an understandable key roles & responsibilities, does not ensure the company will succeed. This is just the beginning, they still need to plan and execute.

With the beginning of most businesses you will find a business plan. Or at least that is what the traditional school of thought has been. But as we have evolved and as business has evolved rapidly more professionals are going the route of skipping the business plan. The rationale behind this is:

1. I don't have any revenue coming in
2. The market is changing rapidly
3. I'll evolve to my customers changing needs

Sure, you want to have an idea of what you want to do. But the old-school method of having a demographic profile of you client and financial projections are starting to die away. However, if you are trying to get funding from angel investors then they will want to see that information, but more than likely you have already started the business and have some hard numbers to back it up.

What does all of this do with you? I want you to start thinking like you are a business. When I look at my household I like to call it Meyers Inc. Now there are things that we do well and areas that we need improving but I know that if we stay disciplined, Meyers Inc will be successful.

To think like you are a business you need to set benchmarks that you can use to compare yourself at different points in the future. Remember we are in a race to crush debt. As you continue to read I want you to start feeling nervous, a little anxious, but mainly excited because you can do this. We are now starting to lay the foundation for how you are going to track yourself going forward. There will a system of accountability, everyone will have a role in the household. As you learn more about the workings of your household it will start to run like a finely tuned machine. So, strap on your running shoes because here we go.

Balance Sheet
The first step is getting a snapshot of where you are currently. Depending on how well organized you have your financials this might take some time initially. Going forward you will want to have a process in place so that

all your financials are in one place. This can be a filing cabinet, if you prefer to handle everything with paper, or simply an excel spreadsheet that you update once a month if you prefer to save things electronically. Other will prefer to use software such as Quickbooks or Quicken. There are also free programs like www.mint.com that can help manage your finances.

Businesses will generate a balance sheet because it provides a snapshot of their finances at a point in time. From this balance sheet, they can gather important information. This can be used to see if the company is still heading in the right direction or if changes need to be made. This is also used by lending institutions and investors to see how well the company can handle their current financial obligations. The information you will need to gather is broken down into several categories: Cash & Cash Equivalents- This is considered highly liquid investments with maturities of 3 months or less. Since most individuals don't have short term corporate bonds or treasuries it breaks down to:

- Cash on hand-Money in your wallet, secret hiding spot, and change jar
- Checking accounts
- Savings accounts
- Money Markets
- Certificate of deposits

Brokerage accounts- Any taxable money held with an online broker, financial advisor, or through an employer (stock purchase plan)

- Stocks
- Mutual Funds
- Municipal bonds
- Government bonds
- Corporate bonds
- Other

Retirement accounts

- 401(k)
- 403(b)
- 457
- IRA Roth
- IRA Traditional
- Profit Sharing
- Pension

Property- Any big purchase items you own that may have value attached to them. You can always use www.zillow.com to find the value of your home and www.kbb.com to find the value of your car

- Primary residence
- Secondary residence
- Rental property
- Investment property
- Vehicle 1
- Vehicle 2
- Recreational Vehicle
- Boat

Short-term credit-Despite the name, which is misleading, this is any revolving lines of credit or fixed loans that will be paid off in less than one year

- Credit card 1
- Credit card 2

- Credit card 3
- Loans from friends or family
- Home Equity Line of Credit
- Other

Loans and Mortgages-This is any fixed loan longer than a year in duration

- Primary residence
- Secondary residence
- Rental Property
- Investment Property
- Vehicle 1
- Vehicle 2
- Recreational Vehicle
- Boat
- Student loans
- Business loans
- 401(k) loans

Other Liabilities-

- Charitable commitments
- Other
- Other

Below is an example of a simple spreadsheet that you can copy or do your own variation. The key point to remember with a balance sheet is just to do it at the same point every single time. You can do it once a year like this example, just make sure it is always done on the same date. You can do it quarterly or even monthly if you find that useful. This will give you an indication of whether you are heading in the right direction.

Assets		
Cash & Cash Equivalents		
Cash on hand	$	100.00
Checking accounts	$	5,000.00
Savings accounts	$	6,000.00
Money markets		
Certificate of Deposit		
Other		
Total Cash and Equivalents	$	11,100.00
Brokerage Accounts		
Stocks	$	600.00
Mutual funds		
Municipal bonds		
Governmen bonds		
Corporate bonds		
Other		
Total Brokerage	**$**	**600.00**
Retirement Accounts		
401(k)	$	20,000.00
403(b)		
457		
IRA Roth		
IRA Traditional		
Profit Sharing		
Pension		
Total Retirement Accounts	**$**	**20,000.00**
Property		
Primary residence	$	260,000.00
Secondary residence		
Rental property		
Investment property		
Vehicle 1	$	24,000.00
Vehicle 2		
Recreational Vehicle 1		
Boat		
Total Property	**$**	**284,000.00**
Other Assets		
Loans to friends/family		
Life Insurance Cash Value		
Jewelry		
Furnishings		
Antiques		
Collectables		
Other 1		
Other 2		
Total Other Assets		
Total Assets	**$**	**315,700.00**

Liabilities		
Short-Term Credit		
Credit card 1	$	4,000.00
Credit card 2		
Credit card 3		
Loans from friends/family		
Home Equity Line of Credit		
Other		
Total Short-Term Credit	**$**	**4,000.00**
Loans & Mortgages		
Primary residence	$	220,000.00
Secondary residence		
Home equity loan		
Rental property		
Vehicle 1	$	23,800.00
Vehicle 2		
Recreational vehicle		
Boat		
Student loans		
Business loans		
401(K) loan		
Total Loans & Mortgages	**$**	**243,800.00**
Other Liabilities		
Commitment to donate		
Other 1		
Other 2		
Other 3		
Total Other Liabilities	**$**	**-**
Total Liabilities	**$**	**247,800.00**
Current Net Worth	**$**	**36,200.00**

Net Worth Over Time		
Year 1	$	15,000.00
Year 2	$	22,000.00
Year 3	$	36,200.00
Year 4		
Year 5		

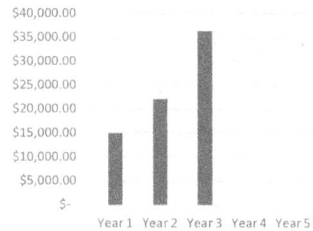

Ideally, we want to see the graph look like steps leading to your goal, if you are fortunate enough to be in a stable job your entire life that process will be easier. In this example, Bob has made modest steps to increasing his net worth. He isn't making a huge leap from year-to-year which is typical unless there is a windfall or a huge surge in the stock market.

Finance can be like losing weight. It isn't a straight arrow to our goal. There will be times when you hit a plateau and you must change things up. There will be times when you have a moment of weakness and you decide to go for desert. The key is to realize what you are doing, modify your behavior, and make changes. The scale is a way to measure your progress, so is looking at your balance sheet. If the balance sheet is going down and it isn't from a onetime event than it is time to reconsider what is happening.

Cash Flow Statement
You now know where you stand. You may have a negative or positive net worth currently, that isn't important, what is important is to have a starting point to measure your progress. This is just the beginning of you becoming a finely tuned business. The next thing we need to figure out is how our cash flow impacts our balance sheet. Before you start having your eyes glaze over from business jargon. This is simply looking at the money coming in compared to the money going out. We want to know where the money is going to make planning more useful in the future.

Initially, I want you to do this every single month for at least 6 months. After the 6-month time frame I want you to assess how you are personally handling your finances. If you feel like you have a good system in place then it is allowable do this quarterly. However, you will want to continue with the balance sheet as a checks and balances system for measuring your progress. If some time goes by and you feel like you are not paying attention to your expenses then it is helpful to revisit this process monthly.

Now this will be tedious, especially if you haven't carefully tracked your spending before. Some of the big bills will be easy to track. You know about your car payment, you mortgage, and student loans. However, when it comes to living expenses they aren't as easy as you think. If you use a credit card to make all your purchases then you will have to break out the statement and individually go through each charge and put it in its proper category. If you come into this exercise with existing debt than just create a credit card category to put those payments. Below is a sample cash flow statement.

Bob Jones	Jun-17	Outflows		
Inflows		**Payroll deductions**		
Income		FICA/Social Security/Medicare	$	400.64
Salary	$ 5,000.00	Federal tax	$	949.00
Interest & Dividends	$ 10.00	State tax		
Social security		401(k)	$	250.00
Retirement income				
Gift		**Debts**		
Tax return		Mortgage	$	1,600.00
Other	$ 400.00	Vehicle 1	$	360.00
Total Income	$ 5,410.00	Vehicle 2		
		Credit card 1	$	250.00
		Credit card 2		
		Consumer loan	$	126.00
		Student loan	$	240.00
		Living Expenses		
		Auto care	$	50.00
		Auto fuel	$	200.00
		Child care		
		Clothing		
		Discretionary	$	64.36
		Food- groceries	$	150.00
		Food-dining out	$	150.00
		Gifts		
		Insurance-auto	$	100.00
		Insurance-life	$	20.00
		Insurance-other		
		Utilities	$	300.00
		Other (specify)		
		Savings Allocation		
		Short term savings	$	100.00
		Mid-term savings		
		long-term savings	$	100.00
		Total Outflows	$	5,410.00
		Difference	$	-

Please note that you will always want your inflows to match your outflows. Even those who are very meticulous may come across situations where there is a difference. Rather than spending countless hours on that missing money just put it into the discretionary category.

More than likely it was just some spending money that you forgot to account for. If the dollar amount is substantial than certainly spend some time going through your account trying to figure out where the money went. You don't want to make it a habit of not accounting for large amounts of money. As a business, we want accountability for spending.

I encourage everyone who is trying to eliminate debt to keep a spending journal with them. This is a forced way to track all that discretionary spending that you do. We will also set limits on the amount of cash that you withdraw from an ATM. The point is to force you to have a method of accounting for your spending. This alone can save people money as they must look at their spending on their checking account.

Now we are well on the way to success, you know where you stand, you have an idea of how your money is being spent. Now the last step is to find out if you are profitable as a business.

Profit and Loss Statement

Now we get to the point where we find out if you are profitable for the year. This will tell us if you spend more than you make or if you are running a surplus. This will look like your cash flow statement. If you have been keeping track of your cash flow statement this will be easy to put together. The profit and loss pulls all the inflow information from the cash flow statement in addition to the expenses that experienced.

When you are reporting information on your personal profit and loss statement just do it on net basis. This means after taxes, medical, and retirement have been deducted. If you are self-employed, unless you W-2 yourself, you will want to report on a gross basis with your deductions listed as expenses.

This report is done typically once at the end of the year, but you can do it quarterly as well. If you have been doing your cash flow statement you will have a pretty good idea of how you are doing financially. It is important to still do this report because it will give you a good idea of how you are spending your money. Only when you know will you be able to properly predict future spending behavior. This will allow you to make behavioral changes in your either your spending or your earnings.

Below is an example. Again, this can be done on paper or you can easily put it into an excel spreadsheet like I have done here.

Revenue	
Salary (net)	$ 40,804.32
Passive income	$ 4,800.00
Other	$ 4,000.00
Total Revenue	**$ 49,604.32**

Expenses		
Mortgage	$ 19,200.00	39%
Car	$ 4,320.00	9%
Credit card	$ 2,000.00	4%
Consumer Loan	$ 900.00	2%
Student loan	$ 2,880.00	6%
Car care	$ 1,200.00	2%
Fuel	$ 2,625.00	5%
Discretionary	$ 4,000.00	8%
Food-groceries	$ 1,750.00	4%
Food-Dining out	$ 2,000.00	4%
Insurance-auto	$ 1,200.00	2%
Insurance-life	$ 240.00	0%
utilities	$ 4,150.00	8%
Total Expenses	**$ 46,465.00**	94%

Surplus/Deficit	$ 3,139.32

In this example, it looks like Bob is spending about 94% of his income. We know that he was putting some money into savings every month. Looking at his monthly cash flow statement it is more than likely that the balance was put into a savings account. We also don't know how much money he started with in his checking account. This surplus will give him some room in case a minor expense arises.

Now we have our budget but how do we know if this is good or bad? While everyone is different we can look at national averages. The Bureau of Labor Statistics provide a survey called "Consumer Expenditure Survey". This provides a break-down on spending based on different demographics. The break down is divided into age, income, family size, education level, race, and other forms of measurement. What the "average" of all these groups tells us is the following.

Category	% of overall spending
Housing	24%
Utilities	8%
Food	14%
Clothing	4%
Medical/Healthcare	6%
Donations/Gifts to charity	4%
Savings & Insurance	9%
Entertainment & Recreation	5%
Transportation (payment, gas, care)	14%
Personal debt/misc	12%

This can be used as a benchmark, but that is all you want to use it for. Please keep in mind that there are several factors that influence these percentages. If you are single than you will spend less money on food than a family of five, but probably more on dining out and entertainment. This will be the same as utilities. If you are on either coast there is a good chance that you are spending a higher proportion of your income on housing.

As you age amount of money spent on medical tends to increase.

If you live in a city and you decide to have a car you will probably pay more than the average because of parking and maintenance cost. The same can be said if you have a large truck for work or to haul a fifth wheel, boat, or another trailer. It isn't unusual for large trucks to cost $60,000 or more. If you decide to finance that it could be a large expense depending on how much money you make.

Just comparing the two we see that housing automatically sticks out as an item that is proportionately higher than the national average. If Bob could get his house down to the national average of 24% he would save over $11,000 per year. This would be more than enough money to make a big dent on any outstanding debt, and put more money away into a retirement or savings account.

Since we are just looking at his financials without knowing more information about Bob, we don't know if this is feasible for him to accomplish that. If Bob lives outside pricey San Francisco than he is in a great position where he probably has a lot of equity in his house. However, if we find out that he lives outside Omaha than he probably has more house than he can really afford and should consider more reasonable options.

One item that is missing from Bob's profit and loss statement are medical expenses. This could be because he is young and didn't have any major-medical expenditures. When you are dealing with a tight budget it is easy to see how a major-medical event could throw, even the best laid financial plans into ruins. This is where an emergency fund becomes critical.

Great, we now have information, and information is power. It is what we do with this information that is going to be the most useful. We can change the direction of our financial future and make a positive impact. Now is the time to act and a big part of that is being in the correct frame of mind.

Budget: A mathematical confirmation of your suspicions-A.A. Latimer

Budgeting is a b*tch

Think big and don't listen to people who tell you it can't be done. Life's too short to think small-Tim Ferriss

Warning, I must use the "B" word, that is right, budgeting. I can see the reactions already, just like in old scary movies, I see a woman shrieking as people are starting to flee the city, heading anywhere unwilling to face a budget.

Settle down and let's talk about what a budget is and what it is isn't. A budget is simply a guideline to use in your spending. Remember we are trying to crush debt, and we need to set guidelines in how we spend our money. Remember this is your business, imagine if a business decided to operate without an operating budget. Marketing would push as many ads as possible, manufacturing would have the latest and greatest equipment, and human resources would hand out benefits and pay raises without a second thought. While it sounds fantastic, this would lead to a company that would quickly go bankrupt. We need to set parameters on how we use money in our daily lives.

A budget is not a chain that you are tied to the rest of your life. Too many people think of it as a confinement that prohibits you from enjoying life. I imagine they see themselves in a budget prison, a cruel form of solitary confinement. That is not what a budget is meant to do, a budget is a tool to set you free. A budget is a tool used to motivate you and provide you with guidance in your financial life. Initially you will be asked to do a monthly budget, but as you progress in your finances and learn healthy financial habits you can revert to quarterly check-ups to make sure you on the right path to success.

A budget has two sides. If you recall from our cash flow statement we have inflows and outflows. To set a proper budget, we must know both sides and how we can manipulate them to get the results that we want. Next, we will cover both sides of a budget and how to create one built for success.

Outflows

Outflows are the expenses that we experience and these will fit into two categories, fixed and variable. Fixed expenses are items that don't fluctuate from month-to-month. Unless you are in a variable rate loan a fixed expense would include:
- Mortgage/Rent
- HOA/Condo Association
- Car payment
- Property taxes (if paying monthly)
- House/Car/Life/Health insurance
- Utility bills
- Personal loans

These are examples of fixed expenses. These "fixed" expenses can change from year-to-year. We know that property taxes go up, insurance changes, utilities rise, along with other fees. But the idea is that you have certainty on how much you are paying. Depending on where you live your utilities may vary from month-to-month unless you are on a fixed program. However, most utilities vary a little each month and you generally have a sense of what they will cost.

Variable expenses on the other hand can vary greatly each month. Depending on the time of year and your social activity these can vary by hundreds or even thousands of dollars. Variable cost includes:

- Groceries
- Personal care
- Medical care
- Fuel
- Clothing
- Daycare/babysitting
- Dining out
- Entertainment
- Tobacco/alcohol
- Sports and recreation
- Gambling
- Children's lessons
- Discretionary spending
- Travel/vacation
- Gifts

Some of these items will vary a little each month, while some will change dramatically. If you are planning a vacation, then even the best laid plans can go astray as you may spend more on dining out, alcohol, recreation, gambling, and other areas. Even if it a vacation with the kids you know the temptation is there to check out more tourist traps, go to the amusement park, and buy more gifts.

Even when you aren't on vacation just having a friend stop by for a weekend or an invitation to play golf can add expenses that you weren't expecting. Therefore, it is important to track your expenses so that you can start planning for the unexpected. When you complete your profit and loss statement this will give you a good idea on exactly how much you spend in each category. With that information budgeting becomes easier. Also, the more you complete the exercise the more precise you can be with your budget.

Let's go ahead and start to work on a budget. Since Bob has been so great about sharing his financial information let's go ahead and use him as an example. Bob has gone through the exercise of looking at his spending and while he would like to reduce his housing expense he is in a good neighborhood and his mortgage is at a fixed rate. Bob also received news that he is getting a 3.5% pay raise, this will raise his salary to $62,100. We know that this will automatically decrease his housing expense per year as a percentage of his pay.

In addition, since starting this practice Bob has looked to cut expenses in other areas and found by bundling his home and auto insurance with another carrier he will save approximately $300 per year total. $200 off his auto insurance and $100 off his insurance. Property taxes did go up but just enough to offset the savings from his house insurance going down. All the other expenses are expected to increase with inflation, which is approximately 2%.

Bob's income will increase because of the pay raise. He had a renter in his house that he was charging just $400/month for a small space in his basement. This year he increased the rent to $450 to help offset the increases in utilities. Bob is probably having too much deducted from his check each pay period since he received a tax refund of $4000 last year, he is expecting a similar return this year.

Looking at Bob's situation we know he has the following fixed expenses.

Income			Monthly
Salary (net)	$	42,232.47	$ 3,519.37
Passive Income	$	5,400.00	$ 450.00
Total	$	**47,632.47**	$ **3,969.37**
Other	$	4,200.00	

Fixed Expenses			
Mortgage	$	19,200.00	$ 1,600.00
Car	$	4,320.00	$ 360.00
Student Loan	$	2,880.00	$ 240.00
Insurance-auto	$	1,000.00	$ 83.33
Insurance-life	$	240.00	$ 20.00
Utilities	$	4,233.00	$ 352.75
Total	$	**31,873.00**	$ **2,656.08**

We are going to set aside the tax return money for now. While this can be reasonably projected, we don't want to include it in our monthly budgeting because this will be one time injection of money. Bob already plans on paying off his credit card balance of approximately $2,000 when he gets his return. In addition, Bob found out he must have reconstructive knee surgery after he tore his ACL skiing. He called his insurance company and found that with his current insurance he will have to pay $5,000 out of pocket. He plans on using the balance of the tax return and his savings account to cover the cost.

While enjoying the single life for several years. Bob recently got into a serious relationship and he has discovered that his entertainment costs have increased along with his dining costs. He plans on increasing his discretionary income and dining budget by 50% this year. He projects his variable expenses to look like this:

Variable Expenses		Monthly	
Consumer loan	paid off!		
Car care	$ 1,224.00	$	102.00
Fuel	$ 2,677.50	$	223.13
Discretionary	$ 6,000.00	$	500.00
Food-groceries	$ 1,785.00	$	148.75
Food-Dining	$ 3,000.00	$	250.00
Savings	$ 2,400.00	$	200.00
Total	$ 17,086.50	$	1,423.88

Bob is excited, he feels like he has a workable budget until he realizes that there is a discrepancy between his income and his expenses. While it isn't a huge difference if he sticks with his current budget he will run a deficit of $110.59/month. While his existing savings and checking, balance would cover the difference, it doesn't get him closer to his goals. He decides to reevaluate his budget and cuts back on discretionary spending $1400. He also wants to look at what is in his discretionary spending so he can be more accountable. This is what he has come up with:

Dicretionary		Monthly
Carrying cash	$ 600.00	$ 50.00
Christmas	$ 1,000.00	$ 83.33
Vacation	$ 1,500.00	$ 125.00
Gifts	$ 500.00	$ 41.67
Recreation	$ 1,000.00	$ 83.33
Total	$ 4,600.00	$ 383.33

While it is a rough idea of what he will spend, this will give him a good starting point in his budget. Remember the key behind a budget is to provide a guideline of expenses. I'll let you in on a secret, it doesn't always work, in fact it rarely works how we want it to. But having a budget is lot better than wandering around without one.

With the breakout that Bob provided of his discretionary spending, he knows that some of that money isn't needed right away. Instead of leaving it in his checking account. He will move it to his savings account where there will be less temptation to spend that money. In fact, one of the easiest things Bob can do is set-up an online savings accounts that pays a higher than normal interest rate and isn't attached to his current bank. This would require a couple of steps to move the money, giving him time to pause about the actual need for the money.

Again, we have a lot of information. Unless we know what to do with this information it is completely useless. Too many times I have talked with people who spent a lot of time working on developing a budget, many times these budgets were developed with wishful thinking and complete disregard of historical spending habits. They have this beautiful budget and after being frustrated they wonder why their budget doesn't work. They still can't save, they are paying overdraft fees, budgets simply don't work they will declare.

The question of how they managed their budget will generally bring a stare. I will ask them how they decided they could withdraw money that caused them to get overdraft fees. Every single time they will say they pulled up their account information from an ATM, they saw a balance and withdrew some money. But what about the budget?

The budget is a tool but like all tools it must be used properly to work. Having a budget and not knowing how to use it is akin to having a wrench but not knowing how to fix a leaky pipe. The pipe continues to leak water and people are asking you "why don't you fix the pipe?" Instead you just lean back and say, "don't worry, I have a wrench."

A budget is a lot of upfront work, I get it, you might spend an hour or two, possibly more on it the first year. This is generally just a fraction of the time people will spend planning for vacation. Depending on the survey you believe most people will spend 10-20 hours per year on gathering information for an upcoming vacation. This doesn't even count the travel time to your destination and back. A vacation will give you a lifetime of memories, but a properly planned budget can assure you a have a lifetime of vacations to take.

It is easy to not do the hard work that needs to be done. But if you do what is easy your life will be hard. But if you do what is hard your life will be easy. Do yourself a favor and do the hard work upfront so you aren't nearing retirement trying to figure out how you are going to survive.

When you have your budget together construct it in such a way so that any "leftover" money shows-up in your checking account. All the money that is already accounted for goes in subaccounts. Remember the examples in this book are exactly that, examples, this is your budget. You know what you spend money on so make a budget that works for you. If you love to golf, then have a golf budget, if you love to read comic books, then have a comic book budget. Set-up categories that work for you and your life.

Checking Account		
Main Checking	$	200.00
Mortgage	$	800.00
Car	$	180.00
Student Loan	$	120.00
Insurance-Auto	$	41.67
Insurance-Life	$	10.00
Utilities	$	176.38
Car Care	$	51.00
Fuel	$	111.57
Groceries	$	74.38
Dining	$	125.00
Carrying cash	$	50.00
Recreation	$	41.67
Total	**$**	**1,981.67**

Savings		
Main Savings	$	7,000.00
Christmas	$	25.00
Vacation	$	62.50
Gifts	$	20.84
Total	**$**	**7,108.34**

By setting-up the account this way you can reference to your budget and that will tell you how much money you should spend on certain categories. Bob went ahead and put the "carrying cash" category into his budget which is a smart move. Instead of even looking that he has $1,981.67, he knows that he can withdraw $50 for cash. Also, since Bob gets paid twice a month this is how he set-up his budget, he simply took his monthly total from each category and split it into half. When Bob gets his second paycheck for this month he will go ahead and add in the second half to each category.

The budget won't always work as planned but don't view this as a failure, instead find out why the budget didn't work. If you live in a cold climate maybe your heating bill goes way up November through March. That is why we deal with averages. If your budget is $353 for utilities, and you spend $300 during the summer, leave that "extra" $53 in the utilities account. You don't have to empty each subaccount, account for fluctuation.

If you spent $350 dining just be aware of it and take corrective action. Being the good son Bob decided to take his mom out for a fancy dinner on Mother's Day and that cost $125. Otherwise he was close to being on target. Bob will have to plan around holidays more going forward and eat at home a little more. The budget is more telling about our behaviors than almost anything else. If a category continues to be a problem than an adjustment might be needed to his budget. Our budget will change just as our lives change and we need to adjust for that. The key to make sure we balance at the end of the month.

Inflows

So much attention is given to the outflows of the budget that people fail to account for the inflows. I have worked with families that want to have one person home so they can watch over their young children, and I am all for it.

However, they will cut their budget to the bones and when it comes time to find more money that is still their solution.

While they do a fantastic job at not having debt they will have a car with mechanical issues, major upgrades to their home that keep getting delayed. They'll be in a phone plan that doesn't fit their family needs, cut back on cable, not go on vacation. While I advocate for such behavior when you are trying to crush debt. When you have one side of the equation completely under control, why don't you look at the other side and try to increase the inflows?

Almost every article out there mentions not having your daily latte, or cutting the cord with cable. Few mention on how to increase your income to meet your needs. Everyone who is reading this has the capability to increase their income, it may not happen immediately but you can increase your income this year if you want.

Before we get into suggestions on how you can make extra money. The first solution is to ask your employer for a pay raise. The worst thing they will tell you is "no", but they might let you know what is required to make more money. This could be additional certification, training, or more responsibility. The solution may be closer than you realize.

With the use of technology there are so many ways that you can make money working from home. While there is still a time commitment, why not add a little extra coin to your pocket and help to ease the pressure on your budget. The first place you should look is at yourself. What skill set do you have that can set you apart? While the initial reaction is, I don't have one, the reality is we all do. My sister, for example, made extra money reviewing grants for non-profits. This is a skill set initially she viewed as a job, she didn't realize that a lot of non-profits need help and oversight when they receive grants. I have a colleague who works in a financial office but is passionate about fitness. She sells supplements and other fitness related items in her spare time. Both opportunities helped to generate thousands of dollars in additional income each year. The more effort they put in, the more money they made.

There are hundreds of ways to make additional money, right at home, this list just a few of those opportunities:

1. Write a blog. If you have an interest in a subject there is probably a following out there for it. If you aren't sure what that interest are, just think about what you rant and rave about most often. This could be politics, entertainment, business, food, boating, education, exercise, your lawn, or countless other subjects. Believe me there is a niche of individuals out there that are just as crazy about a subject as you are. You make your income from affiliate commissions, Good AdSense, and sponsored advertisers. If you

haven't checked out my blog yet make sure to subscribe at www.ignitedaboutfinances.com

2. I mentioned affiliate marketing. You can do this with any blog or website that you have. With affiliate marketing, you simply promote an item that you believe in and ideally have tried yourself. When someone clicks on your link to buy that product than you get a share of the purchase price, this is your commission for helping to sell the product. There are a lot of great websites.

- Rakuten Marketing, this has been named the number one affiliate marketer by mThink for 6 years in a row!
- Ebay Partner Network- A trusted website, this allows you to earn a commission on the items you promote on Ebay
- Shareasale-wide selection of items to choose from
- 2Checkout- This firm focuses on promoting software from thousands of companies
- Amazon-Huge company with thousands of products to choose and promote
- Many more

Keep in mind that if you are selling a product, affiliate marketing can be a great way to promote your brand and get it in front of a new set of eyes. I think you'd be OK giving up a small amount of the selling price to get thousands of potential new sales.

3. Set-up an online store. If you can make almost anything there is a market for it. The most prevalent website right now would be Etsy. I know personally I have ordered jewelry, a blanket, and other items. There are literally thousands of items from small producers all over the world. Whether it is clothing, organic baby care, bottle openers, or a blanket you can get a unique item that isn't sold at big box stores. You can also check out online stores for:
   - Amazon
   - Ebay
   - Zazzle
   - CafePress
4. Find freelance work. While many of the jobs can be related to writing, the skill set required varies greatly. The company or person requesting the work could require a skill set in accounting, engineering, translation, legal, and other categories. A good website for this would www.upwork.com
5. Write a non-fiction eBook. I promise I will get off the writing kick here but it is an excellent way to make extra money. If you think you can't write my advice is to simply start. An eBook doesn't have to be long but the content should be worth reading. Simply start writing and develop a way to get followers. I know several people who have made several thousands of dollars without any effort in promoting their book. However, to make

consistent money create a following and release a couple of books.

6. Drive for Uber or Lyft. We have a love affair with our cars and if you have a good driving record and a car that meets their qualifications you can use that car to earn extra money. There are many people, including parents who take advantage of these programs. I know a mom of three young children who makes about $200 a week driving for Uber, she doesn't drive a lot, mainly in-between errands and a little in the evening when her husband is home. The $800 does makes a big difference in their ability to pay bills. If you have an older vehicle and it doesn't qualify to carry passengers, you still can drive using Ubereats to deliver food.

7. Rent out a spare room with AirBNB. If you have a spare room you can rent it out using AirBNB. AirBNB allows you to require ID verification so you know the person who is staying with you is who they say they are. This is all done before a person can book your room. In many cities, you can rent out a room for $50 or more per night, what a great way to make an extra $1500 per month. If you are willing to give up a little privacy it is a solid income generator and a great way to meet people from all over the world.

8. If you are already a parent why not offer babysitting. What a great way for your child to have a play buddy and for you to make a little extra coin. Every parent needs some time off and

once you are known as a trusted provider you will have all the work that you can handle.

9. If you want to work for an actual company there are many that offer positions geared toward busy parents. Many of these positions are geared at professionals helping to keep their skills sharp while raising little ones. Thank you to www.thespruce.com for this list:

- www.flexjobs.com
- www.thesecondshift.com
- www.powertofly.com
- www.prokanga.com
- www.ratracerebellion.com
- www.flexforceprofessionalsllc.com
- www.momproject.com
- www.corpsteam.com
- www.hiremymom.com
- www.flexibleresources.com
- www.flexibleexecutives.com

Beyond these companies there are many more that offer virtual assistant positions. Your job would be to answer customer service calls from the comfort of your home. Just make sure you have a dedicated quiet space and a schedule that you can keep.

10. Want to get out of the house? There are several companies that local part-time positions that are geared toward second shift or third shift schedules. The bonus is that many of these companies will provide health insurance after working a set number of hours and provide other

bonuses. There are companies that can help you get in shape, lose weight, and make extra money such as FedEx, Costco, and UPS. If physical work isn't your thing there are positions at JP Morgan, Lowe's, and Starbucks that offer part-time work with benefits.

11. If you just need an injection of money you can always hold a yard sale or sell items on Craigslist to clean out your house. There is also the option of holiday work. It is easy to find part-time work during the holidays and if you work at a store that shop at frequently this can be a bonus as you will likely receive an employee discount.

Whether it is office work, retail, construction, or management there is always an option to make additional money using your current skill set and perhaps learning a new one. Some of these could eventually replace your current job. More importantly this will provide a much-needed boost to your income and completely change the outcome of your budget.

Going beyond your budget this can literally change your entire financial future. We will look at Bob's situation, by all accounts it looks like he is a younger man with simple needs now. His outlook could change based on family, career, and several other factors. If we assume that Bob stays on his current career track, and that he is 32 years old, and that he just started contributing 5% to his 401(k). With a 50% match, up to 6%, Bob would have $845,789 at retirement with a consistent 7% return. Not bad, but in today's dollars it isn't going to be a whole lot of money for Bob to rely on. He will also have social security, but the future of that could be in question.

However, if Bob worked a side hustle making an extra $5,000 per year (adjusting for inflation) and put that money into his 401(k) his balance would be $1,841,566. That extra $5,000 adjusting 3% each year for inflation works out $288,650.88 additional money that he could put away, but the result is an extra million dollars for retirement. I am sure that Bob is glad that he put the time in for a side hustle to save for his retirement.

While a lot of people take this to heart I know there will be the detractors who say they don't have the time for any of the items I listed, even though on average Americans spend:

- 5 hours and 4 minutes watching television per day
- 1 hour and 39 minutes a day consuming media on their phone
- 31 minutes a day consuming media on their tablet
- 8 hours sleeping and on personal care
- 8 hours and 8 minutes working or traveling to work

These are average so please stop writing the angry email about your specific situation. The reality is that there is more time during the day than you realize. You have a choice in how those hours are spent. You can watch your favorite show, or you can take steps to make more money. You can play games on your phone or you can make more money. You can sleep eight hours or get six hours, and make more money. The people who are financially secure and successful don't have special traits that you don't have, they are simply more efficient with how they spend the hours they have.

I love this quote from Arnold Schwarzenegger:
I've always figured out that there were 24 hours a day. You sleep six hours and have 18 hours left. Now, I know there are some of you out there that say well, wait a minute, I sleep eight or nine hours. Well, then, just sleep faster I recommend.

If you are still complaining, saying I NEED those eight hours I ask you to think back, whether it was high school, college, travel, or whenever it was that you had to get less than eight hours of sleep. How were you able to get by? You probably had something pressing that needed to be done, whether it was a paper to finish, a flight to catch, or work that needed completed by a deadline. You had something to do, something that needed to be done.

To reach your goals, you need to wake up and be energized about what you are doing. Make the most of the hours you have because they are never enough. And then know there is a so much to accomplish that after 6 hours of sleep the next night you jump out of bed. These are your goals, your dreams, I can't help you achieve them unless you take the first step and get up earlier.

One thing you will notice as you go through the process of establishing a budget is that the more effort you put into inflows the more you will dictate the outflows. However, if you are constrained with an income that can't fluctuate, use the budget as a range to work with. Every month look at areas you excelled and what you need to improve upon. After a while it will be a good habit, and eventually the occasional check-up will be needed.

You now know where you are, where your money goes, whether your business is profitable, and how to set a budget controlling the inflows and outflows. You can succeed, however there is a huge emotional equation to money and that needs to be addressed.

A healthy relationship will never require you to sacrifice your friends, your dreams, or your dignity-Mandy Hale

The Company You Keep

Staying in an unhealthy relationship can keep a person from finding their own way and moving to the next level of their own path-and that person could even be you. Sometimes the best way to save someone is to walk-away. Real love sometimes means saying goodbye-Bryant McGill

We are in a race to eliminate debt, while debt can happen for a variety of reasons we must take a hard look at what happened initially. Some of the fixes will be minor and they can be worked through by looking at your current spending, your income, and establishing a budget. Through hard work and persistence, you will be in a position where any debt is eliminated and you are comfortable living within your means. You will feel the relief, the burden, that debt has on so many be lifted. When you are free you will realize that you can fly, you can achieve what you want to, you do have a bright future.

For others, the process needs to go much deeper. They have been to financial professionals in the past, they have worked with debt counselors, they have read the books and took a pen to paper to create a budget. On the surface, they are doing all the right things but something isn't clicking because they are right back in the same situation.

If you are in a situation like that, or you have been struggling for a long-time it is helpful to know that you aren't the only one and there is help. Depending on the stress level that you are experiencing you may need to seek professional help, it is known that bad stress at a high level can reduce resilience against mental health problems.

When I mention, mental health problems, it isn't full flown problems like schizophrenia, but problems in your ability to make sound mental decisions. This can lead to other issues such as failed marriages, lost homes, and even suicidal tendencies.

When I want you to crush debt this just isn't a phrase but a mission to help as many people as I can. The spiral that comes from debt can be swift and sometimes painful, but there is a help.

Denial is one of the mental health problems people experience. You will notice this occurring when someone refuses to open their mail or answer phone calls when they fear it is a creditor. They may also deny the amount of their debt even when they have a statement or other proof. There will times that a credit card is maxed out and they will simply open another credit card. This is a protection mechanism, almost like living in an alternate reality. A side effect of too much bad stress.

Fear and panic will also begin to set in. The thought of a bill being paid late or facing another fee won't just bring disappointment but outright panic. This include dizziness, shortness of breath, shakes, and even a headache. This is also known as anxiety. 40 million American suffer from anxiety and financial stress can be a big trigger to bring out the disorder.

Anger is one of the scariest disorders that someone can experience. This disorder doesn't just affect them but it affects everyone around them, and in rare cases causes physical harm. Instead of internalizing what is happening someone will start to look to external sources to place their blame. They will blame the economy, their boss for not paying them enough, their spouse for not making enough, their kids for costing too much, the creditor for sending bills, and even angry at themselves for getting in this situation. If this isn't enough, anger places additional stress on your body leading to migraines, heart disease, and your body's ability to fend off disease.

Depression is the most recognized disorder associated with debt. Depression can lead to low self-esteem and suicidal tendencies. However, it also reduces our ability to resist piling on more debt. Instead of taking extra steps to reduce debt someone who is depressed will treat themselves to feel better. This can be a shopping trip, vacation, or a fancy dinner. While this temporarily provides a release, depression quickly sinks back in once the euphoria wears off.

There is hope, there is a light at the end of the tunnel, sometimes the journey will be long and challenging, but not more than you can handle. Sometimes it requires bankruptcy but you need to start working with someone now if you or someone you love is experiencing any of the above symptoms. Because the end goal is to get to that last find step, and that is relief, and having everyone get to the best version of themselves.

If you are aware of the disorders that financial stress can bring, you are ready to make a change, but you still feel in a rut then it is time to look around you. As with all challenges in life it is easier if we have a healthy support system around us. This is obvious in everything we do. A solid support system is instrumental in achieving resounding success. While it is fun to read stories of the lone wolf who was successful in achieving success, that is also why those stories make the news, it is rare.

Behind almost successful endeavor is a mentor, a supportive spouse, or a great friend. If you have found yourself in a situation where your finances are spiraling out of control, stop what you are doing and ask yourself the following questions:

- Am I changing my behavior to control my money?
    - What steps have I taken?
- Have I sought outside help?
- Am I solely in charge of my finances?

If you have answered those questions "yes" and you still aren't making any progress than we need to go back to the beginning. This is your business, we want you to succeed, but we need some accountability. Start over with the cash flow statement, go back three months. Pull up your credit card and bank statements. Be very precise about where your money is going. How much money is being spent on discretionary items? Furthermore, by spending money on discretionary items how much is being spent on interest every single month. Go ahead and add it all up from every source you have (exclude mortgage). This includes credits cards, vehicles (include ATV's, boats, jet skis, etc...), payday loans, and bank overdraft fees. How much does that total? Is it $500, $1000, $1500? Whatever that total amount is write it down on a piece of paper. Don't just use a small portion of that paper, make it huge, and now post it somewhere that you can see every day. Think about what you could do with that money.

As you think about what you can do with that money look back at how you are currently spending your money. Are you receiving the satisfaction from that purchase that you thought you would? If you could do it over would you change your spending from the previous months? What would you like to purchase with the money you are currently using to pay interest?

This is a serious look inside yourself. If you find your spending is related to shopping, dining, and socializing. It is also important to look at your friends and ask yourself if they are helping you get any closer to your goal. This is also a two-way street, if your friends are unaware that you are trying to get out of debt and you continue to act in a way that would lead them to believe you have more disposable income than you do, you are culpable.

If you recall from the introduction, I turned my situation around when I took ownership of my debt and let my friends know about my situation. Instead of shunning me as some people are concerned, they embraced my challenge and helped me to take steps to succeed. This included them helping me find a second job, finding less expensive ways to hang out, and staying supportive. If your friends do anything differently than it is time to find new friends. As harsh as that sounds, they really aren't your friends if they don't support you in a time of need. What you need most is emotional support with the changes you will have to go through. Good friends will stick with your through thick and thin, not just when times are good.

If you answered "yes" to two of the questions but you aren't solely in charge of your finances. It is important to go through the same process as before. Really look at your spending, where it is going, and what steps have been taken to control your situation. After this evaluation, you need to look at where the spending is coming from and who is responsible. This isn't to place blame but to determine if both members are on the same page.

Almost always, shared accounts are the results of a spouse; however, I do see it with parents and their children as well. If it is your spouse who has spending that is out of control and you are taking steps to correct your family's situation there are several steps that need to be taken.

1. Make sure your spouse is aware of the severity of the situation, they should go through the balance sheet, cash flow, and profit & loss statement with you. They need to be aware of the goals and have some buy-in. After that, put together a budget <u>together</u> so you have an accountability system in place.

2. If you have gone through that process and your spouse's spending is still out of control, it is time to put them on an allowance. There isn't a problem with this, in fact later in life I learned that my dad had an allowance. My mom did the books, she let my dad have a set amount of money and that was it. They did discuss their finances but it was a way to limit discretionary spending.

3. Seek counseling. If you have gone through why you need to get out of debt, limited spending, and your spouse continues to show reckless behavior it is time to seek help. A counselor can help to uncover the real reason behind the spending. This could be because of child hood experiences with money. Either coming from a family that never had to worry about money or coming from one that never had any. With the help of a counselor they can help to uncover the reasons behind the behavior and steps to improve it.

4. If your spouse's reckless behavior continues, start to separate your financial life. If you recall there are several disorders when it comes to financial

stress. If you stay in a relationship that is unhealthy for you financially it is literally killing you from the stress. If your spouse refuses through all the other steps to make changes it is going to take you down financially as well. While I would never advocate getting a divorce you must consider that finances are with you the rest of your life. Unless this is just a temporary mid-life crisis not controlled by therapy, the choices made financially will affect everything you do. This includes going on vacation, holidays, retirement, education for children, and even where you live. By separating your finances this means separate checking/savings accounts, and credit cards. If you already cosigned a loan there is little than can be done but to pay your share. This will provide you peace of mind for your financial situation and steps to make sure you are independent.

    a. A side note, if you do go through the steps of a divorce it doesn't mean that you won't be liable for paying some of your spouse's debt. By having most of your finances separated and showing financial prudence, a judge will likely be sympathetic and assign debt proportionately. If your spouse racks up a lot of debt after you file for separation, you aren't held liable for that amount. That is why it is important to get credit cards, lines of credit, and other debt out of your name. This includes all joint accounts where it would be difficult to prove who spent the money.

When you marry someone, you don't just marry the person, but also their finances. Most couples are supportive of each other and will be able to develop a game plan together. When you have a team, you can get momentum with each victory, and with each milestone. Soon, with you and your spouse working together you can accomplish all the goals, you'll also discover a better relationship by working together.

If you have a joint account with someone else pay close attention to why you have that account with them and if there is equal benefit for the ownership. I'll see these many times when a parent has a joint account with their child. If you are financially supporting your child you need to understand when it is time to cut the cord and let your child support themselves.

This will often start during college and continues, sometimes indefinitely, as their child "finds their true calling", or you are "just helping them out until they are on their feet". I understand that parents want to help their child but you aren't helping them by subsidizing their life. Your child needs to grow-up and by allowing them to syphon money from you, it isn't teaching them any life lessons. We all want to have a job that we are passionate about and that fulfills us, but not all our jobs are going to do that. Furthermore, you may not truly know what you are passionate about until you start trying different occupations. You can make a good living doing anything! The first step is trying out different jobs and not becoming reliant on mom and dad.

If the last paragraph struck a chord with you, making a change isn't easy. If you are the parent it can be heartbreaking to have the conversation with your child how you are cutting them off. If this has been happening for a while, they begin to feel entitled to the money, that somehow because of your hard work and effort they deserve the money. It will most likely be an emotional conversation and not always well received. You can't risk your financial health and retirement because of your child. Even if you can afford to, you want to raise an independent child who is a contributing member to society.

If you are the child, you can stop swearing at me now, it is time to grow-up. I am not saying that your parents can't help you at all. But relying on their money for your livelihood isn't fair. Your parents gave up a lot for you, they have spent years of time, a lot of money, and a lot of emotion to get you to where you are. I promise they want you to succeed and I know you want to make them proud.

I love this quote by Sylvester Stallone from the move Rocky Balboa. He is talking to his son who is blaming Rocky for how difficult life and work is because of his name:

Let me tell you something you already know. The world ain't all sunshine and rainbows. It's a very mean and nasty place. And I don't care how tough you are. It will beat you to your knees and keep you there permanently if you let it

You, me, or nobody is gonna hit as hard as life, but it ain't about how hard you hit, it's about how hard you can get hit and keep moving forward, how much you can take and keep moving forward. That's how winning is done.

Now if you know what you are worth, go out and get what you are worth, but you gotta be willing to take the hits and not pointing fingers, saying you ain't where you want to be because of him, or her, or anybody. Cowards do that, and that ain't you. You're better than that.

I am always going to love you no matter what, no matter what happens. You're my son and you are my blood, you are the best thing in my life. But until you start believing in yourself you ain't going to have a life.

A better option in this case is to provide an allowance during college and slowly cutting back as your child graduates and begins their career. If you want to provide a large amount of money to your child, a better option than a lump sum would be to open a trust that pays out a limited amount per year. You can also set this up so that bonuses are paid out when your child hits certain milestones. While I've been accused of being overly harsh at times the reality is that there are many students who get by in college without any financial help. Some parents will even have them maintaining a job as a requirement to continue getting financial help from them. However you decide to proceed, make sure there is a game plan to cut back and assist your child, not develop an entitled adult.

The race to eliminate debt isn't easy alone, but you don't have to go at it alone. You are surrounded by loved ones who are eager to help you. If they don't support your dream than you need to distance yourself from them. Just as one bad apple spoils the bunch, one bad friend, relative, or other influencer can ruin your attempts at financial freedom. I can't express how important it is to have a positive network around you and eliminate the negative. At the end of the day you are ultimately responsible for the decisions you make, the debt you have, and for you the financial condition you are in, and the friends you keep. You can try to blame someone else but if you continue to let them have control over your life, pull you into bad decisions, you are just a culpable as they are. Make the decision today to eliminate the negative from your life and propel yourself further. You can't soar with someone dragging you down.

A big part of financial freedom is having your heart and mind free from worry about the what-ifs of life-Suze Orman

Victory-Paying off the debt!

Victory belongs to those who believe in it the most and believe in it the longest-Randall Wallace

The business of you is set-up for success. You now have a system in place, you have your balance sheet to get progress reports on your overall financial health. You have cash flow statement to show exactly how you are spending your money. This helped you to create a sustainable budget to live by. You did a profit and loss statement to make sure your inflows can keep up with the outflows. More importantly you recognized that money and debt is an emotional experience. The stress from debt can cause disorders to your mental health making it more difficult to accomplish your goals. By being aware you can make steps to successfully address those. Most importantly you have been taking steps to eliminate negative people in your life, because believe me you are worth it.

Getting the foundation in place is critical to having success so that you can eliminate debt. The question then becomes what is the best way to eliminate the debt? This is where I am more liberal than some of my colleagues. My answer is the fastest way possible and by any means (well legally any means). A lot of this must depend on you, this is where soul searching comes into play. You must understand yourself, your limits, and your tendencies. This will only be successful if you are honest with yourself.

Going cash only

If you are someone who's tendency it is to spend, shop till you drop, and sees the limits on credit cards as extra money than you will need to go cash only. This often works best when someone has a professional to assist them. The reasoning is that going cold turkey on anything is not easy. A professional can help you by putting money in buckets, or jars in this case. The same idea behind our budget, we have so much allocated for living expenses and a little fun.

By going cash only, you will be forced to live on 70%-80% of your paycheck while the rest goes to debt payment. This 70%-80% includes living expenses, usually leaving very little discretionary money. Having someone there to make slight modifications to your budget is helpful, in addition they can check your bank and credit card statements to make sure there isn't any "cheating" going on.

This is not easy but for some people but it is required. This tough love will be an adjustment at first but eventually you adapt to living on less and enjoy the success you see. Many professionals will have you cut up or hand over their credit cards. Unless there is an emergency reserve someplace than you will want to keep at least one credit card. This will serve as a lifeline in case of an emergency.

This is a great system, it eliminates temptation of spending on credit. More importantly it helps to serve as a reminder that the money you are spending is real. It is a lot different spending $40 on a meal by handing over cash instead of simply sliding a credit card. The habits you make will stay with long after you finish paying off your debt.

Debt Snowball

This method was made popular with Dave Ramsey, and I happen to like this method. The idea behind this philosophy is that you list all your debts from smallest to largest.

1. $1,200 credit card #1
2. $2,000 credit card #2
3. $9,800 credit card #3
4. $12,500 car loan (3-year loan)
5. $20,000 student loan (10-year loan)

Next you will want to look at the budget you established. It is critical if you are dealing with debt to apply as much as possible to the debt without causing financial stress elsewhere. Let's say after you did your budget you only had $500 to apply to debt and this included your student loan and car loan, this is causing you to run a deficit each month. Knowing this wasn't enough you decided to get a part-time job at FedEx working the second shift unloading boxes. This job pays you approximately $1,000 per month. You use this money strictly to pay down debt.

Now you have $1,500 earmarked for debt payment. With this method, you pay the minimum payment on all the debt besides the first one, the first one gets the minimum plus what is left over from your budget. So, your payment schedule might look like this.

1. $669
2. $40
3. $196
4. $364
5. $231

You can see that your first debt will be paid off within two months. Once you finish paying off the first debt your payment schedule would look like this.

1. $709
2. $196
3. $364
4. $231

You continue to do this so the amount of money going to each debt increases like a snowball being rolled. Eventually you will have $1,500 going toward your student loans and start living the debt free life.

From a financial point of view this may not make the most sense logically (we will talk about that next). Remember that the relationship that many of us having with money is an emotional one. If you can pay off a debt in a short period of time it can give you an incredible lift. This emotional burst of endorphins can lift your spirits and bring you focus as you tackle the next debt. With each successive victory, it brings more excitement and the positive feeling of accomplishment.

Debt Avalanche

The debt avalanche will be a faster way to pay off debt but may not bring you the victorious feeling right away. The premise is the same, you list all your debts, except this time do it from the highest interest rate to the lowest:

1. 19.9% credit card #3 ($9,800)
2. 12.9% credit card #1 ($1,200)
3. 10.9% credit card #2 ($2,000)
4. 6.8% student loans ($20,000)
5. 3.1% car loan ($12,500)

We still have our same $1,500 pot to work with in paying off our debts. This method will pay it off more quickly because the highest cost debt is eliminated first. In doing this process though you aren't seeing an immediate victory. The payment schedule will look like this:

1. $841
2. $24
3. $40
4. $231
5. $364

With all the hard work done it will still take 14 months to pay off this card. When someone is paying their bills, psychologically, that can be a long time for them to not see a victory. Instead they see themselves sending in check-after-check to the same companies. In the end, they know this will work in their favor but the emotional boost isn't there with this method.

<u>Controversial-The Balance Transfer</u>
If you have gone through all the steps and even got a part-time job to help pay your debt, I know that you are serious. I'll assume you are also monitoring your credit with a free service and know your credit score. If you have a credit score of 690+ there is a good chance that you can transfer all or most of your credit card balances into another credit card with a 0% interest for a set period.

This is often anywhere from 12-18 months even though I have seen some go as long as 21 months. Most will have a balance transfer fees that are roughly 3%. There are some important things to note when doing a balance transfer:

- Pay off the entire balance before the grace period expires. If you have any remaining balance after the grace period you will be charged a much higher rate.
- Never forget a payment! Most balance transfers eliminate the 0% grace period if you miss a payment
- Don't charge up the credit card(s) that you just paid off
- Resist using the new card to make purchases

Does a balance transfer make sense for you? Let's look at the math, we will assume that the balance transfer is 0% for 15 months with a 3% transfer fee. We will simply do an analysis for the credit cards. There are some cards that will allow you to consolidate car loans but given the limited resources to pay off the debt and the fact that the car loan is almost 3% currently it wouldn't make sense.

Debt	Amount	Current Interest	Amount per month to pay off in 15 months	Total Spent
Credit card #1	$ 1,200.00	12.9%	$ 87.05	
Credit card #2	$ 2,000.00	10.9%	$ 143.23	
Credit card #3	$ 9,800.00	19.9%	$ 743.33	
Total			$ 973.61	$ 14,604.15
Consolidated	$ 13,390.00	0.0%	$892.67	$ 13,390.05
Savings				$ 1,214.10

If you can put $1,200 in your pocket by doing a balance transfer responsibly, I am all for it. This would help you to pay your credit cards off in the fastest manner and save money. Also, since you did the math ahead of time you know you could put $905 per month toward the consolidated debt, instead of the $892.67. While you wouldn't pay it off in less than 15 months, the last payment would be about $175 less, and you could use that money to help pay down your student loans (or celebrate with a night out).

The concern that other professionals have is that you are essentially exposing yourself to abuse more credit. While this is a valid concern, if you have gone through the steps above and taken a serious look to see if this is the best option for you, then go with it. This will provide you with $1,200 that would have gone toward interest, now it can go toward paying down the principal on your student loans!

Controversial-HELOC or cash-out refinance

Another option is to use the equity in your house to pay off your debt. This can be a great option but it comes with a lot of warnings. If you recall from the beginning of the book when you have a mortgage the interest rate is lower because it is a secure loan. This means that if you are unable to make payments to your mortgage than you are in danger of losing your house. You have also been through a process to eliminate your debt, and if you can do it quicker, cheaper, and more efficiently that is what we are all about.

What is difference between the two? A HELOC or home equity line of credit works like a credit card. Based on your credit score, income, and the equity in your house you will have access to a pool of money for generally 10 years. For example, the lending institution after looking at everything determines you are eligible for $50,000. You don't have to take out the $50,000, it is there when you need it and you only pay interest on the money you borrow. Most lenders will require an initial draw, for example if you qualify for $50,000 they might have an initial draw of $30,000 that is required. After the initial draw, there isn't a requirement. Also, HELOC's are variable interest, this means that the interest rate fluctuates with a benchmark. This benchmark is often indicated by prime plus a percentage. Prime is the most widely used benchmark and is the rate that banks will lend money to their most-favored clients. This rate will move in lock step with changes by the Federal Reserve Board.

A cash-out refinance is a new mortgage altogether replacing your current one. Lenders will typically allow you to borrow up to 80% of the equity in your house. For example, if your home has appreciated to $250,000 and you only owe $125,000 you could refinance and borrow up to $75,000. This was calculated by taking $250,000 times 80% which equals $200,000, once you pay off your current lender you are left with $75,000 (less fees). With this you get a lump sum of cash instead of a pool of funds that you can draw from.

There is a third option worth noting which is the home equity loan. This is like the HELOC in that it is a second mortgage instead of replacing your main mortgage. With a home equity loan, you get a lump sum of money instead of continued access to a line of credit. These aren't as prevalent as they used to be as the HELOC has replaced them. However, you can still find them and they do offer an attractive option for those needing a lump sum of money. These loans generally have terms from 5 to 15 years

As with all debt we want to make sure we are using it responsibly, so just because we have access to more money than we need doesn't mean that you should take it out. In this case, we are going to look at a HELOC. This will provide us with the flexibility to take out the money we need and provide an emergency fund if we don't have one. Lending institutions still must approve you so make sure your credit is in good shape before you apply.

Since you are in the race to get out of debt we will want to compare rates. You can go to a website like www.bankrate.com that compares multiple lenders side-by-side. Many of these sites have the credit score that is required to get a loan listed next to the rates. This will provide you with a good indication whether you will qualify. Looking at current rates they vary from 3.74% to 7.25% but we will assume that you get 4.9% on your loan.

Just because a site has the lowest interest rate doesn't mean that it will be the best for your situation. In addition to the interest rate you want to find out the following:

- What is the minimum draw? This is the amount you are required to withdraw when you open the account.
- Is this just an introductory rate? You may be lured by a small percentage but if it increases after 6 months or a year it may not fit your situation
- How much are the lender fees? Some banks will charge a fee when you establish a HELOC.
- Is there a required balance? Some banks will require a certain amount of the balance be used at all time. This is added interest expense that isn't needed.

- How much is the annual fee? A lot of banks charge a fee ranging from $50 to $200 every year just to maintain the HELOC. Try to find a bank without one.
- Is there a cancellation fee? A lender may charge you a fee to close your account if you haven't had it for a set period, these costs generally range around $300. In addition, they may have closing cost recapture, since some lenders don't charge a fee when you establish your HELOC, if you haven't held it for two years they will charge you those fees at closing.

Ideally you want a bank that doesn't charge any closing cost, doesn't have an annual fee, and doesn't have a minimum required balance. If you found these, you really aren't concerned about a cancellation fee or closing cost, because you can keep the HELOC open without any fees.

Now we must get into our analysis, one thing to remember is that the interest on a HELOC is tax deductible. This means that at the end of the year you get some of that money back in your tax refund, or it at least decreases the amount of taxes that you must pay. This also must be considered when we do this analysis, this number will vary for everyone. Whether you do your taxes by yourself or have them done by a professional you will have an idea of your tax bracket. For most people, it will be in the 25% range, keep in mind that this is your federal tax rate. In addition, you also pay consumption taxes, local taxes, and state taxes.

Sometimes the state taxes are in the form of fees, property tax, or other methods to make up for a lack of a state income tax. If you felt that 25% was too low, you are correct, the actual rate is much higher when figuring all taxes and fees.

First, we will look at just paying off the credit cards:

Debt	Amount	Current Int	Amount per month to pay off in 15	Total Spent
Credit card #1	$ 1,200.00	12.9%	$ 87.05	
Credit card #2	$ 2,000.00	10.9%	$ 143.23	
Credit card #3	$ 9,800.00	19.9%	$ 743.33	
Total			$ 973.61	$ 14,604.15
Consolidated	$ 13,000.00	4.9%	$895.25	$ 13,428.75
Savings				$ 1,175.40

For the credit cards going this route would save you over $1,100. Plus, the $428.75 in interest that you paid with the HELOC is tax deductible. If your tax rate is 25% you would get approximately $107.19 back in your tax return. When you include this, it saves you money over the credit card balance transfer method.

We can also look at consolidating your student loans as well. Since we have a budget of $1,500 per month toward debt payment and a car payment of $364 we will have to stretch out the length of the repayment, for this example we did 36 months which is also when the car will be paid off.

Debt	Amount	Current Int	Amount per month to pay off in 36	Total Spent
Credit card #1	$ 1,200.00	12.9%	$ 40.37	
Credit card #2	$ 2,000.00	10.9%	$ 65.38	
Credit card #3	$ 9,800.00	19.9%	$ 363.70	
Student loan	$ 20,000.00	6.8%	$ 615.71	
Total			$ 1,085.16	$ 39,065.76
Consolidated	$ 33,000.00	4.9%	$987.56	$ 35,552.16
Savings				$ 3,513.60

Consolidating all the loans into a HELOC will save you over $3,500! We are assuming interest rates remained steady the entire time, however even if interest rates did rise you will still see savings. It is highly unlikely that interest rates could rise enough to make this scenario not effective. Over the three years you paid $2,552.16 in interest, with tax rate of 25% you would reduce your tax liability by approximately $638.04. The total tax and interest savings is over $4,000, that is actual money that you can use to save or invest.

A side note to using mortgage interest deductions in your calculations is that not everyone itemizes their taxes and receives that tax break. A little less than half of all homeowners don't receive the benefit of mortgage interest deduction because they take the standard deduction while doing their taxes. Look at last year's returns to determine if including the deduction makes sense in your situation.

While not advocated by many, why work longer and pay more interest than is necessary. In these examples, we assumed that you had good credit. If your credit has suffered because of missed payments, consolidating your debt into credit cards or a HELOC may not be an option. You could look at personal loans, but unless all your credit cards have interest rates in the 20%+ it likely won't make sense.

Don't be discouraged, keep grinding, no one ever said this was going to be easy. Keep working and you will start to pay down your debt and your credit slowly starts to improve. Once it improves enough you can take advantage of these strategies to become debt free.

During this process, you will become hungry for freedom. Everything you look at will become a method to decrease debt. If you have a spare room you will rent it, if you have extra toys you will sell them, if you have expensive memberships you will cancel them. The reality is that the extra $1,500 per month to cut down debt will become $2,000 and potentially more as you realize the opportunities around you.

The sense of accomplishment at the end is unbelievable. You will find that the dream trip you could never afford is now within reach. The fear of balancing your checkbook is no longer a chore. Trying to make all the payments every month is no longer a juggling act. Financial freedom is within reach, but you must want it. You need to know your why. Why are you doing this? Is it for your retirement? That dream vacation? Your children? Your spouse? Once you understand your why use it every day to propel yourself forward. Once you crush debt you will feel like you can conquer anything in life. You deserve this. You deserve a life of freedom.

Today I close the door to the past, open the door to the future, take a deep breath, step on through and start a new chapter in my life-unknown

What's next?

If you have a dream, don't just sit there. Gather courage to believe that you can succeed and leave no stone unturned to make it a reality-Roopleen

Congratulations, you are well on your way to living a life of fulfillment because of your ability to handle finances, crush debt, and accomplish your goals. Once you have accomplished those goals what are you going to do?

It will still be vitally important to keep a budget and keep a check on your finances. Just as someone who lost a lot of weight can fall out of good habits, so can someone who has experienced debt and climbed their way to victory. You will have choices to make once the debt is paid off, you can use that money to save and invest, or you can use the money to increase your discretionary spending.

The reality is that you will likely do a little of both. You have fought the good fight and you deserve to get a reward from it. Take some of that money and spend it on something that you enjoy. This can be extra money for vacation, concerts, going out to dinner, golf, remodel, favorite hobby, or to have extra carrying cash. The choice is really yours, that is the beautiful part of a budget, it is designed by you for you.

Part of that money must be put away for a rainy day. There are two essentials that you will have to save for.

Emergency Fund

You have probably heard the name before, but what exactly is an emergency fund? This is a fund used in case of a severe emergency. The one most often brought-up is losing your job. This can also include accidents, medicals bills, and other unforeseen expenses.

The amount you should have in your emergency fund really depends on your situation. You will hear 6 months of living expenses as a common answer. If you are the sole bread winner for your family and the only source of income then this is a good goal to aim for. If you have ever worked with someone who is solely responsible for paying the bills, putting money away for retirement, saving for vacation, and then ask them to put 6 months of money away for emergencies, it isn't going to happen. Sometimes they are lucky if they can go on vacation.

If you have a dual income family than the number drops down to three months of living expenses. The thinking here is that the likelihood of both individuals losing their job at the same time is small and there will be at least one paycheck.

For those who are self-employed and rely heavily on cycles in the economy than one year of living expenses should be saved. The individuals that this will impact the most include mortgage brokers, realtors, luxury sales, and other positions that can see extreme highs and lows.

Instead of being overwhelmed by the number just put a little bit of money away with each paycheck. Ideally this will be in an account that is difficult to access. As you get tax refunds, bonuses, inheritance, or other unexpected income go ahead and put some of that in the emergency fund. It may take years for you to fund this account but simply be consistent with funding it. When you look at it every so often you will be surprised by the growth you see, and it will provide comfort knowing that there is money that you can fall back on.

Retirement Savings
It is critical to start saving for retirement as early as possible. Simply relying on social security to provide you for retirement isn't going to be enough. In fact, social security usually provides about 30% of what you were making during your working years. The more money that you make the less that social security will provide for you as a percentage of your income. You must supplement social security with your own money.

If you are young in your 20's or 30's than aim for 10% of your income going away toward retirement. As you get older you will have to put more money away to get a similar income. If you haven't started saving please start today. According to the Economic Policy Institute (EPI) you should have 8 times your salary saved by the time you turn 60. But the median amount saved for ages 50 and 55 is only $8,000! This is not a case where you want to be average.

You are going to work forever! I have heard this before, but 60% of all retirees retired earlier than they expected. This can be a result of health challenges, laid off, or caring for a spouse. This isn't a time to take chances and assume you will be the 40% that gets to walk away when they want. I wouldn't be surprised if the 60% number is higher as people will often fail to disclose something that they are embarrassed or ashamed about. Instead start putting away some money today.

Take some of that money and invest it in yourself and your retirement. This will be money well spent. If you are looking for ideas on how to save money, invest, or plan a proper portfolio make sure to check out my upcoming books and check out my blog at www.ignitedaboutfinances.com.

Inner peace begins the moment you choose to not to allow another person or event to control your emotions-Pema Chodron

Final Thoughts

We live in a society obsessed with social media and celebrities. The next time you go outside look around and observe how many people have their heads buried in their phones. I'll admit that I do that at times as well. We live in a world where people have this misperception about how everyone else lives. We do it one picture at a time. We scroll through our Facebook feed and see smiling faces on vacation. We see a glass of wine framed against a beautiful sunset. We see a new car being driven for the first time. We start to compare ourselves to those images, the highlights of someone else's year to our daily routine.

This isn't reality, what society has become is a picture, a catch-phrase, and a meme. A society that judges too quickly, rarely knowing the whole story. Do yourself a favor and stay away from that life. I am not saying to get off social media, many people use it to connect socially and for business. I am saying be the best person you can be every day, in the real world, and don't compare yourself to the illusion of someone else's.

The success belongs to those who are grinding hard every single day to accomplish their goals. There isn't a magic pill that will take care of all your problems. Self-discipline, doing the correct things day-after-day is the only cure.

There will be struggles, no one ever said this would be easy. In fact, you will make mistakes, and then you will make more mistakes but when you fail, fail forward. Never be afraid to make mistakes, because the second we stop making mistakes is the second we stop growing as individuals.

Failing forward is the ability to get back up after you've been knocked down, learn from your mistake and move forward in a better direction- John C Maxwell

You may be overwhelmed; the mountain of debt may appear too high to conquer. What you need to do is focus on the next step. Don't look up at the mountain, just focus on your next step. What can you do today to make things better? Then focus on the next step, stay grounded, and keep working. Then focus on the next step, and before you know it the mountain will be conquered. The decisions you make today will affect your future. This includes the decision to wake up early, the decision to eat properly, the decision to exercise, the decision to spend wisely, the decision to make more, the decision to get out of unhealthy relationships. Take ownership of your life, don't make excuses, now is your time. Ignite the fire inside and crush the debt.

It is not the mountain we conquer, but ourselves-Edmund Hillary

About the Author

Matthew Meyers is a business owner who has started, and sold, various businesses during his lifetime. His true passion has always been about helping others. He can fulfill that passion through personal finance. He has counseled thousands of individuals and couples in their pursuit of better financial management.

With a degree in business from Western Michigan University, an MBA, and his certification as a Certified Financial Planner™ Matthew uses his education and experience to coach his clients. An avid reader, he stays on top of trends (good and bad) that influence the behavior of his clients.

With a thriving practice and constant development of new products to assist his clients, Matthew looks forward to everyday and the difference he can make.